John Blackman was born in Melbourne in 1947 and began his showbusiness career in 1969 at 2GN Goulburn. Since then, he has become well known through radio shows on 2CA, 3AW, 2UE, 2GN, 3UZ, 2GB and 3AK.

However, he is probably best known to millions of Australians as 'the voice' of the highly successful and anarchic, ad-lib weekly Nine Network variety show, 'Hey Hey It's Saturday'.

Blackman and his alter ego, Dickie Knee, have been an integral part of the show since its inception twenty-seven years ago.

Blackers lives in Melbourne with his wife, Cecile, and daughter, Tiffany.

aussie
GAGS

OVER 1400 OF MY
FAVOURITE ONE-LINERS
AND JOKES

JOHN BLACKMAN

Pan Macmillan Australia

First published 1998 in Pan by Pan Macmillan Australia Pty Limited
St Martins Tower, 31 Market Street, Sydney

National Library of Australia
cataloguing-in-publication data:

Blackman, John. 1947– .
Aussie gags.

ISBN 0 330 36097 3.

1. Australian wit and humor. I. Title.

A828.802

Typeset in 11/16pt Bembo by Post Pre-press Group
Printed in Australia by McPherson's Printing Group

Acknowledgements

I would like to thank all my friends, relatives, acquaintances and show-biz colleagues who not only contributed quite a few jokes, but helped jog a chardonnay-ravaged memory on many more.

Special gratitude, though, goes to my darling wife of twenty-six years, Cecile – who has recently confessed that she never actually married me for my looks or my money – she married me because I made her laugh.

I hope to continue to do that for the rest of our lives.

Contents

Foreword

Many years ago, somebody much older, wiser and more talented than me once said, 'Amateurs imitate, professionals steal'.

If that is the case, then this book represents an unashamed litany of larceny, misappropriation, pilferage, plagiarism, robbery and thievery.

Over the twenty-eight years I have been involved as a performer on both radio and television in Australia, I have been privileged to work with many famous and gifted performers . . . and they know who they are.

During this time, God has blessed me with an ability to store one-liners (in what passes as my brain) and to be able to blurt them out just at the right time. Some people call it a gift; others just call it being a smart-arse.

Whatever it is doesn't really matter. The ability to make people laugh is a joy and, as the cliché goes, it really is the best medicine. Not only that, I am firmly convinced it keeps you young, hence the tragedy of this juvenile delinquent trapped inside a pathetic fifty-year-old body.

This book contains no doubt many jokes you've probably heard or read before but, as another *even* older, wiser person once said, 'There's no such thing as an old joke – just a new audience'.

And, of course, it's not the joke, it's how and when you tell it. Not every one-liner and joke is 'laugh out loud' funny, so I am relying on you to use accents where appropriate and the odd vulgarity or profanity if necessary.

You will note that I have avoided using the f★★k word (I use my quota up each week playing golf) as I've always maintained, to get a laugh, a good joke teller should never have to stoop to swearing or profanity. It is, after all, the refuge of the ignorant and the inarticulate (apart from that, my mum will probably read this and, even at my age, I'm not too old to cop a clip under the ear).

Use this tome wisely (it can be a lethal weapon in the wrong hands) as an aid for all sorts of occasions – weddings, bar mitzvahs, funerals . . . anything. Enjoy!

My Favourite One-liners

We had a great neighbourhood watch going when I was a kid . . . until she closed her curtains.

He's what every woman wants – strong, sensitive . . . battery operated!

There is no truth in the rumour that Roy Rogers's horse Trigger sued him for palomino-mony.

Chap with a fetish walks into sex shop and asks: 'So how's the leather been lately?'

The latest product on the market in the continuing war against white ants – it's called 'Arson'.

Unfortunately, since I went on the wagon, the wagon went and got a liquor licence.

Do infants have as much fun in infancy as adults do in adultery?

Marriage – nature's way of stopping people fighting with strangers.

OK, so God made Heaven and Earth. But what's he done recently?

Graffiti: Dyslexics of the world – untie!

My grandfather died peacefully in his sleep. Which is more than I can say for the three passengers he had in his car at the time.

My friend is so full of self-importance – when he dies, he wants his mail forwarded.

. . . He's also a master of the English language. He's the only bloke I know who can describe Pamela Anderson and Dolly Parton without using his hands!

. . . And he has a very educated palate . . . It's a shame the rest of his head never graduated.

I eat from the three major food groups: McDonald's, Hungry Jack's and Pizza Hut.

I always keep a coathanger in the glove box – just in case I ever lock my keys in the car.

When a girl says 'No' she really means 'Yes', but not with you.

To err is human . . . to really stuff something up takes a computer.

Sure you can't take it with you. But you can stash it where no other bastard can find it.

I can't wait to get really old – then I can actually pick my nose in public.

Dumb? He's so dumb whenever he leaves his car he leaves the windows down so he won't lock himself out.

My father never liked me. As a kid we'd play trains – he used to tie me to the tracks!

. . . And he used to give me bath toys like electric toasters and hair dryers.

My friend is so stupid – he thinks a baby boomer is a kid with flatulence.

When I was a teenager it took me a lot of time to work up the courage to ask the chemist for a packet of condoms. Now it takes me even longer to choose which colour.

Women! First they marry you for your money . . . then they divorce you for it!

I told her I'd take her on an ocean cruise – she said she'd rather a *Tom* Cruise.

My wife says my sex drive has taken up walking.

I told my wife I want die in bed. She said, 'You did last night – three times!'

He's just a bit kinky – only went through nursing school so he could wear white pantyhose.

We were having such a romantic afternoon making love in the back seat of the Mercedes – then they kicked us out of the showroom.

I'm gradually getting my body back into shape – at least twice a week I *think* about doing some exercise.

Loser? He's such a loser he says he was forced to have sex in a hotel room against his will. Problem was he was all alone.

My wife had a sex change . . . Now it's Wednesdays and Saturdays instead of Tuesdays and Fridays.

You know you're losing your figure when you come home and find your husband wearing your bra and panties – and he looks better in them.

Ugly? She's so ugly in the school play she played the hunchback of Notre Dame . . . without make-up.

My mother-in-law told me exercise helps burn off calories. I told her a flamethrower would be quicker.

We have a self-cleaning refrigerator – she leaves stuff in there so long, it eventually crawls out under its own steam.

My psychiatrist says I'm manic-depressive – I have mixed feelings about that.

Every time I walk into a singles bar I can hear Mum's wise words – 'Don't pick that up, you don't know where it's been'.

He was an unwanted child – his parents would give him plastic bags to play with.

Enough is enough – unless, of course, you're a nymphomaniac!

I used to be a great lover – these days the only thing that gets me up at night is my bladder!

Had to get caps for my firm's golf day. Ordered all sizes – large, medium, small and management!

Sign on brothel door: 'Out to lunch – beat it!'

I hate chiropractors . . . they're so manipulative!

He has an inner glow – problem is, it's his liver.

Little-known Sammy Davis Jr hit: 'My Eye Adored You'.

He's about as popular as a flashbulb going off in a motel room.

Just think, in court the defendant puts his life in the hands of twelve people too stupid to get out of jury duty.

Television: living proof that people will look at anything rather than each other.

Time is God's way of preventing everything happening all at once.

I went to Japan with Dad's old translation book. Not much help, only had stuff in it like 'Throw down your weapon'.

So dog is man's best friend – but who wants a friend who drinks out of the toilet bowl!

I'm on a new diet: I eat anything I want and drink a slab of beer a day – I don't lose any weight but it helps me forget I'm fat!

Where else but at the post office do they chain down a pen that doesn't write?

As the old saying used to go in our house: 'Where there's smoke, there's dinner'.

Another great way to annoy her: at the drive-in, when she goes to the loo, move the car!

Life's a bitch – I've just got rid of my acne, now I'm starting to go bald.

Latest thing on the market for the true hypochondriac: the full-body condom.

When I die I'm leaving everything to my kids – I just hope they can afford to keep up the repayments.

Business is so bad I no longer have to keep two sets of books.

You know it's a gay church if only half the congregation is kneeling.

My great uncle Harold joined the circus as the human cannon ball – got hired and fired the same day.

You know you're getting old when the 'snap, crackle and pop' you hear first thing in the morning isn't your Rice Bubbles.

Ugly! He's so ugly he's one of the very few people I know who looks worse than his driver's licence photo.

He once starred in a medical training film about STDs – '*Germs of Endearment*'.

I have a job collecting bleeps and blunders for those television shows. Yes, folks, I'm a blooper scooper!

I hate sushi – just can't bring myself to eat fish they catch other fish with.

My mother-in-law spends each New Year's Eve in a gay bar – just so she won't have to kiss anybody at midnight.

You know the magic is starting to go out of your marriage when the only see-through thing she wears to bed is a hairnet.

His latest girlfriend is so young, on their first date he weaned and dined her.

Definition of divorce: Getting custody of your sanity.

Remember, chase all the happiness you can get . . . Just don't catch anything.

The worst thing about being a proctologist is you start at the bottom and that's where you stay.

. . . Then there was the dermatologist who built his business up from scratch.

Did you know that ninety-seven per cent of men who wear polo shirts can't actually play it?

Lack of money is the leading cause of poverty.

My wife was mad at me last night – sent me to the beginner's end of the water bed.

Television: the thinking man's masturbation.

How tough? Shaves with his wife's razor!

Are Santa's little helpers known as 'subordinate clauses'?

. . . And if he treats the elves badly, is that called 'elf abuse'?

He's so egotistical . . . Collects his own autographs.

A special day for my stupid mate. It's the tenth anniversary of the day he found out the Coyote *never* catches the Roadrunner.

I think my Rottweiler might be gay – caught him listening to a Judy Garland record yesterday.

I have very selective taste in music – I only ever listen to Meatloaf when I'm hungry.

Latest bumper sticker: 'God is a single parent'.

Poor? We were so poor the only way we could keep warm in winter was by passing round a fever.

Latest diet alphabet soup: no vowels.

Messy lover? He was so messy the last motel he stayed in they had to change the *carpet*!

When they made my husband they kept the mould. Pity they threw away the brains.

Being an alcoholic helps him lose weight because he forgets where the food goes in.

Old? He was so old by the time we lit the last of his birthday candles the first ones had burned down.

Looking at my beautifully decorated fish tank I thought, With fronds like these, who needs anemones?

Sign outside divorce lawyer's office: 'Satisfaction guaranteed or your honey back'.

Cheap restaurant: no wine list, the waiter just lets you smell his breath.

Tough restaurant: the waitress has the wine list tattooed on her arm.

Bad restaurant: three parking spaces out back marked 'head chef', 'head waiter' and 'ambulance'.

I once went all the way with a girl . . . then couldn't find my way back.

From the school of the bleeding obvious: the bigger they are, the smaller you are.

Never sit naked on a king-size bed if you have a small penis.

My lawyer can't guarantee to get you off but he will get you a heterosexual cellmate.

I love drinking – it makes me see double and feel single.

In our local gay neighbourhood, the traffic lights go from crimson to peach to lime.

Bad cook? Mum was such a bad cook for Mother's Day we bought her a matching set of fire extinguishers.

Fat! He's so fat he was trying on some corduroy trousers the other day and his legs caught fire.

Hey, great threads. Pity someone's made them into such a bad suit!

He wears today's clothes – shame about his yesterday body.

Bad cook? She's such a bad cook she uses the smoke detector as a timer.

It's time to diet if you look across a crowded room . . . and you're the reason it's crowded.

Ugly? He's so ugly a game of spin the bottle is more like playing Russian roulette.

There was something he always wanted to do when he turned sixty-five – but now he's forgotten what it was.

The ventriloquist's wife divorced him for always snoring on her side of the bed.

If you look like your passport photo – you're too ill to travel.

Building a bomb shelter in your home is OK provided you're home when the bomb goes off.

My wife is a sex object – every time I ask, she objects.

When I die, I want to come back as Demi Moore's bath salts.

. . . Or as Pamela Anderson's icy pole.

Listening to him talk is a bit like playing golf – you have to allow for the wind.

Librarians do it by the book.

What's the difference between hard and dark? It stays dark all night.

What's the difference between light and hard? You can sleep with a light on.

Drunks tend to look at the world through rosé-coloured glasses.

He's got so much gold in his teeth, his mouth fluctuates with the market.

He thinks he has the body of a Greek god – more like a goddamn Greek!

Flew here with Crashlandia Airways – made ten stops, mainly for parts.

Hey, great jacket! Looks just like one they make you wear at clubs when you don't have one of your own.

I could tell the boss was in a bad mood when he lit a cigarette just by holding it against his forehead.

He leads a very ordered life. Works eight hours, sleeps eight hours, eats eight hours (or drinks eight hours).

Little-known blues singer: Urethra Franklin.

Little-known opera singer: Placenta Domingo.

New naval medical training film: *Those Aren't Barnacles Sailor.*

If it costs taxpayers around ten thousand dollars a metre, how come they call it a freeway?

Great news! I've just successfully completed the Doyle Carnergy memory course.

Another way to avoid loneliness: shave your head and sit in the rockmelon display at the supermarket.

She wishes I looked a little more like Pierce Brosnan – I wish she looked a little less like Danny de Vito.

Indian chief teaching young brave places ear to the ground, looks up and says, 'hmmm, buffalo come'.
Young brave says, 'How you know?'
Chief says, 'Ear all sticky.'

My solicitor and his dog are very close – met each other chasing the same ambulance.

Snow White moved out of the seven dwarves' house. Couldn't stand all the small talk.

The Government's latest tax reforms are putting a lot of dollars into the pockets of a lot of people . . . mainly accountants.

He wanted personalised number plates so he changed his name to NYD 456.

Don't ever worry about going bald – remember, good men always come out on top.

Poverty – the perfect tax shelter.

My mother is afraid of mice – she keeps a frozen cat in the freezer.

Ours was a mixed marriage – she was perfect and I wasn't.

My father is a C.P.A. – that's car parking attendant.

As a kid he collected four hundred *National Geographics* – didn't know what to do with them so he became a doctor.

How do you know if your lawyer is lying? His lips are moving.

Without elastic, we would probably take up twenty-five per cent more room.

Our new receptionist is so promiscuous, she deducts her bed as office equipment.

The movie was so bad, they rated it P.G. – puking guaranteed.

Granny finally stopped Grandpa biting his fingernails – she hid his teeth.

Went to a wife-swapping party the other night – got a lawnmower for mine.

Then there was the bulimic's surprise party – the cake jumped out of the girl.

Couldn't sleep last night – tried counting sheep but the smell kept me awake.

Why do Scotsmen wear kilts? Because sheep can hear zippers.

Two funeral parlours have just gone out of business in my home town. Evidently the competition was just too stiff!

Stopped for petrol at a kosher service station the other night – they offered super and unleavened.

My sister never tells a bloke she loves his company unless she's sure he owns it outright.

I asked the librarian for a play by Shakespeare.
'Which one?' she asked.
'William,' I said.

I avoid clichés like the plague.

If naked aliens ever landed here, what bits would we know not to look at?

If our legs bent the other way, what would chairs look like?

I discovered my wife's secret to tender veal – she lets the dog chew on it.

I only smoke after sex now – I'm down to a packet a year.

My friend is so macho he smokes *during* sex.

I'm on the new prune juice marathon diet: eat for a day, run for a day.

As Pamela Anderson once said, 'The Lord giveth and gravity taketh away.'

Fat? He's so fat he's big enough to have his own postcode.

Stupid? He's so stupid he bought a colour telly because he was sick of watching *Casablanca* in black and white.

Orville and Wilbur Wright were the first men ever to fly slower than the speed of sound.

Our dishwasher broke, so we've gone back to the old way – letting the dog lick the plates clean.

It was so cold this morning, when I let the dog back in his leg was still up.

Boring? He's so boring he sat down the other day and wrote his memoir.

Rich? He's so rich he only burns teak firewood.

Mean? He's so mean he joined a nudist colony to save on dry cleaning.

My mother never liked me – used to let me lick the icing off the beaters whenever she made cakes . . . but always forgot to turn off the mixer.

My girlfriend smokes in bed . . . Not bad on the couch either.

Our marriage ended because of religious differences – she worshipped money, I didn't have any!

Dad died in a hunting accident – something he disagreed with ate him.

The doctor told me to drink plenty of liquids and get lots of rest – so I drank till I passed out.

I don't know why they call it 'take home pay' – mine never makes it that far.

Politicians are indeed a rare breed – if only we could find a way to stop them reproducing.

When Mum found out sharing needles could spread HIV she stopped going to her weekly knitting circle altogether.

Celebrity birthday today: Michael Jackson's nose just turned nine.

Skinny? He's so skinny whenever he yawns, his pants fall down.

One good thing about begging (or busking) – at least you're your own boss.

Lazy? He's so lazy he leaves razor blades all over the lawn in the faint hope it might cut itself.

Got a hot date with a grammar teacher tonight. Which is correct? 'May I?' or 'Can I?'

Definition of 'convalescent' in our local hospital is someone who's still alive!

Fat? He's so fat people hang around him at the beach just for shade.

He never treats a woman like an object – but occasionally treats an object like a woman.

The headmaster said my son was illiterate. I'm not surprised, he can't read or write either.

Her: I'd like to get something off my chest.
Him: Like what?
Her: Well, your eyes for a start!

Fat? He's so fat he once bent over in a restaurant to tie his shoelace and the waiter sat a party of six around him.

What about the Siamese twins joined at the hip who went to America so the other one could get to drive!

Guns don't worry me, it's just the bullets.

I'm losing my hair so rapidly, my barber now charges a search fee.

My correspondence school had its reunion recently – everyone mailed each other their picture.

Sure I have thin hair, but who wants fat hair?

One cannibal to another: 'I ate a clown last night . . . tasted kinda funny.'

I hate orgies, I never know who to thank when it's over.

My doctor gave me two placebos and said, 'Pretend to call me in the morning.'

How do you tell the difference between a male and a female gorilla? By the way their shirts button, silly!

Did you hear about the pacifist bullfight? The matador used pillows.

Fat? He's so fat he rents his shade out to mushroom farmers.

His girlfriends are so young, their pyjamas still have feet in them.

He was a total workaholic – at the mere mention of work, he'd go out and get drunk.

Weird? He's so weird he stopped talking to himself recently because of something he said.

. . . I told him my computer was down – he offered to come over and have a drink and a chat with it.

I've got a family physician – he treats mine, I support his.

Husband: I'm my own worst critic.
Wife: Oh no you're not!

Talk about promiscuous, she's spent more time on her back than Michelangelo.

We had a very small wedding – had to throw the confetti at each other.

A gay friend cancelled his trip to London when he found out Big Ben was just a clock.

I broke up with that Polish girl – her name was too difficult to scream out during orgasm.

Ugly? She's so ugly they use her photograph to cure sex offenders.

At school I was voted 'most likely to recede'.

I thought Alcoholics Anonymous meant drinking under an assumed name.

Got into an argument yesterday with a handicapped person trying to park in one of *our* spaces.

Is a guy who has sex ten times a day a spermicidal maniac?

My son plays the piano by ear – he looks so stupid, I wish he would use his hands.

I had such a rough childhood – I got to know my father like the back of his hand.

Unfortunately when she had a facelift there was another one just like it underneath.

I've been sacked from every job I've ever had. At least you can't call me a quitter.

Strange? He's so strange when the other kids were playing doctors and nurses, he was playing vet.

Grandma wants a dignified funeral for Grandpa so she's scrapped that idea of a lucky pew number.

It was so cold this morning, I saw a dog stuck to a tree.

He doesn't smoke or drink – just being alive is his only bad habit.

I have a lot of trouble sleeping – sometimes I'll toss and turn at my desk all day.

Dull? He's so dull last night he went out and painted the town beige.

Latest pick-up line around the jogging track: 'Your pace or mine?'

Dull? He has all the charisma of a soap dish.

They've finally achieved sexual compatibility in bed – they both get their headaches at the same time.

Got sacked from Hungry Jack's last week – dropped a whopper behind the counter.

Sold the car last weekend. Got a pretty good price for it, Avis rent a car weren't too happy though!

Sold the house last weekend. Got a pretty good price for it, although the landlord was a little pissed off.

As Jimmy Bakker once said, 'Evangelists do more than lay people.'

I got thrown out of the baths for peeing in the pool. Everyone does that you say, but not from the high-diving board!

Weird? He's so weird as a child he used to wet the bed . . . from the top of the wardrobe.

He spent so much time standing in the corner at school, he grew up thinking he was a fern.

She was only the stablehand's daughter, but all of the horse manure.

My former wife said she wanted to dance on my grave – I've arranged for a burial at sea.

Dumb? He's so dumb, to count to twenty he has to take off his shoes and socks. To get to twenty and a half, he has to take off his trousers.

The stealth bomber jacket: nobody knows you're wearing it!

Customer: Seventy-five dollars! You're putting me on!
Hooker: No sir, that's an extra twenty-five!

He's such a bad driver – I've never seen a St Christopher medal sweating before.

My home town was so impoverished both sides of the tracks were wrong.

My son ran away from home four times – you'd think he would have got it right the first time.

Fat? He's so fat that as a kid, he got stuck in his hula hoop.

You know how some people can toss a peanut in the air and catch it in their mouth? I do it with soup.

What about the psychologist who used to give his kids mental blocks to play with.

Great meal! But according to my calorie-exercise diet, tomorrow I have to jog one hundred and seventy-five kilometres.

Remember girls, the quickest way to a bloke's heart is through his chest.

My son's teacher must really like him. She's keeping him in her class for another year.

He's such a hypochondriac he has a walk-in medicine cabinet.

He's had his foot in his mouth so often, his tongue reads 'Welcome'.

Science has discovered that death is the number one killer in Australia.

One good thing about having a cold: you don't have to use as much air-freshener in the loo.

My wife used to make toast for me each morning . . . until she lost the recipe.

We couldn't bear to be parted from our cat when she got run over by that steamroller . . . so we use her as a bookmark.

Talk about a neglected childhood, the only way we knew where Mum and Dad were was to listen to the police scanner.

My wife is so loving, last night she greeted me in a slinky negligee, drink in one hand . . . my best friend in the other.

They say people will laugh at anything. So where are they whenever I'm telling a joke?

Ugly? She's so ugly the last time I took her to a horror movie, the audience turned around and looked at *her*.

My mother-in-law went in for open heart surgery last week – they're still looking!

If you're his only patient, it's about time to change doctors.

Archaeologists recently found some totally intact ancient bones. Unfortunately they cannot be disturbed, they're still inside . . . (insert old living treasure's name here).

I finally worked up the courage to tell my in-laws it was time they moved out. Then they reminded me it was actually *their* house.

Whenever he takes a stroll down memory lane he takes a wrong turn and we have to organise a search party.

Her parents knew our marriage wouldn't last – they gave us a twenty-four-piece paper-plate setting.

In the wedding photos all my relatives had mosaics over their faces.

. . . And little black stripes across their eyes.

In our wedding album, all my photos were stuck in face down.

Another great way to get rid of the in-laws: walk around the house naked.

It was so cold today, I saw a politician with his hand in his own pocket.

The road to hell is just like a holiday – half the fun is getting there.

The black eye was a golfing injury – his wife caught him making an easy little five-footer on the putting green.

The latest Jeannie Little doll: it keeps talking even after the batteries are dead.

I went to such a tough school. In art class we learned how to sketch composite pictures.

I went to such a tough school the bus would just slow down to let us off.

Old? He's so old he was a conscientious objector during the Crusades.

My mother-in-law has one very strong point – right in the middle of her forehead.

What's the difference between a fifteen-year-old kid and a fifteen-year-old car? It's easier to reason with the car.

We imposed a midnight curfew on our kids but couldn't stay awake to enforce it.

He was struck off for having sex with one of his patients. Damn shame, he was one of the best vets we ever had.

Talk about fat, his parents always wanted twins, but not in the same body.

. . . No man is an island but, in his case, we'll make an exception.

Another question nobody can answer: if they never shut, how come 711 stores have locks on their doors?

Phone or write to relatives often, it doesn't cost much and beats the heck out of having them over.

He's such a bad driver – I've never seen a St Christopher medal wearing a crash helmet before.

You know you've reached middle age when there's more hair growing out of your nose and ears than on your head.

She's such a bad cook: how can toast have bones?!

The best ten years of my wife's life? Easy. Between thirty-nine and forty!

There should be more policewomen. Why shoot a suspect when you could nag him into giving up?

I took a photograph of my wife in the nude. Well actually, I *was* wearing shoes and socks.

I married the perfect woman. Cooks like her mum, drinks like her dad!

She bought the new sheepdog bra. It rounds 'em up and points them in the right direction.

. . . Then there's the bird–dog bra. It turns setters into pointers!

I told the policeman who arrested me I was just following the instructions on my wife's note: 'Drop pants at drycleaners'.

I promised the doc I'd watch my drinking – so now I only go to pubs that have mirrors.

The bank returned one of my wife's cheques. Now she's wondering what to buy with it this time.

The drought was so bad they had to close down three lanes at our local swimming pool.

Rich? He's so rich he has two swimming pools. One for those who wish to swim and the other is empty for those who don't.

My house is so small whenever I put the key in the front door it opens the back door.

. . . It's so small, you have to go outside to change your mind.

. . . And whenever I paint a room the walls stick together.

Woke up at 2 a.m. with my ear ringing – I was so tired I let it ring three times before I answered it.

Tough? She's so tough she puts her earrings on with a staple gun.

I know an under-achiever, he's spent most of his life in search of the fountain of middle age.

Rich? He's so rich he bought his dog a postman.

So many motorists swear at me, my St Christopher medal wears earmuffs.

He's not fussy, to him a perfect 'ten' is a 'four' who pays for her own drinks.

When my son grows up he wants to be a policeman, says it must be great to have a job where the customer's always wrong.

I had a terrible nightmare. Dreamt I was eating a giant marshmallow, when I woke up my pillow was gone.

Sign hanging on door to assertiveness class: 'Out to lunch – back when I'm bloody well good and ready'.

He's an expert in his field, of course it's only a quarter acre.

He's outstanding in his field, I just wish he'd come in occasionally.

She said she was sick of me, so I bought her a get well card.

The human race is increasing at the rate of three people per second. P.T. Barnum was wrong, there are one hundred and eighty suckers born every minute.

Grandpa loved gardening so much, when he died we put him through his mulcher.

He has no luck – his kidney donor turned out to be a bed-wetter.

I have so little interest in the past, I've had all the rear-vision mirrors removed from my car.

Blonde: Of course I believe in monogamy, I have a coffee table made out of it.

In the ideal marriage no-one wears *any* pants.

I could never be a doctor – tragically, I faint at the sight of golf clubs.

Uncle Wally lost all his money – invested in a battered-fish refuge.

Grandpa loved home cooking so much, we decided to put him in one (a home that is!).

Pit bull terriers really are stupid. The one next door can't tell the difference between a door-to-door salesman and his dinner.

Thrifty? He's so thrifty when his girlfriend told him she was pregnant he said, 'That's the last time I'll use *that* condom!'

Do you think Beethoven's parents ever used to make him play for visitors?

Whenever I drink, I tend to say things I don't mean, like 'Give us another'!

The mother-in-law must be coming to visit – the mice are throwing themselves onto the mousetraps.

My dog is getting so old he now only chases parked cars.

Our cat is dead. I know they're supposed to have nine lives . . . unfortunately the semi had eighteen wheels.

You know you've reached middle age when your knees buckle but your seatbelt won't.

The difference between a weed and a plant? Easy, simply pull up everything, and if it grows back – it's a weed!

You know you're getting old when you have to install a bifocal peephole in your front door.

I failed that mind-reading course – the teacher caught me thinking about cheating.

He's such a bad driver – I've never seen a St Christopher medal wearing a blindfold before.

My wife is fifty – I don't know how old that is in human years.

God in his infinite power and wisdom could have created the world in just one day – he just didn't want us having a six-day weekend.

Ugly? You look up ugly in the dictionary and there's a photo of her.

My new girlfriend's idea of being good in bed is not hogging the doona or snoring too loud.

Old age hasn't affected him at all, he's still the same forgetful, doddering slob he was forty years ago.

Talk about a compulsive gambler, he once lost fifty dollars betting on a merry-go-round horse.

I loaned a mate one thousand dollars for some plastic surgery, now I don't know what the bastard looks like.

I am a picture of health – unfortunately that picture was drawn by Salvador Dali.

Whenever we had a substitute teacher I used to give her an artificial apple.

He wrote a book on building a small business – it ended at Chapter Ten. (Accountancy gag folks.)

Some people have no shame – last week a house guest stole all my hotel towels.

Science says after forty women can still have children. Which is OK if you want forty-one kids!

He can't get a date, so last night he parked at the beach and had car-phone sex.

They laughed at Marconi, they laughed at Edison, they even laughed at Ford. If only I could get in touch with their writers!

Great hospital! When my wife went in for an operation, they gave me a loaner!

My passport photo is so underdeveloped, I'm only allowed into Third World countries.

We finally disconnected the machine my son's been hooked up to for ten years – his Sony Walkman.

I just finished my thesis on writer's block – 500 pages . . . all blank.

Stupid? He's so stupid whenever daylight saving finishes, he puts all the parking meters back an hour.

Parallel lines never meet, however they do maintain extended eye contact.

My imaginary friend died after taking an overdose of placebos.

My friend's what you might call obsessive. Ever met a bloke who flosses his dentures?!

He's got a serve that's harder to get back than your virginity.

We're really worried about our three-year-old – he's acting so childish.

My mother-in-law lands tomorrow – on the world's first wide-body broom.

Why does Chinese food always look as though it's already been eaten?

Squeamish? He's so squeamish when he goes fishing, he sticky tapes the worm to the hook.

I rented a Catholic mass work-out video – stand, kneel, sit, stand, kneel, sit . . .

At Christmas time, dad would deck the halls . . . and then me!

Salvation Army's latest girlie magazine: *Repenthouse*.

My dog has never had an accident inside the house, however he has caused a couple on the freeway.

I'm worried about my pit bull – all the bones he's burying in the backyard are wearing shoes.

I grew up in such a tough suburb you could walk for blocks without leaving the scene of a crime.

My wife changed gynaecologists when she found out he was seeing other women.

My wife is so considerate – she now only throws things at me that are inexpensive to replace.

After two weeks of marriage, I felt like a new man. Unfortunately, so did she!

Husband: I've just been replaced by a machine.
Wife: Funny, that's what I was going to say.

I've just joined Athletes Anonymous – whenever you get the urge to exercise, they get someone to come over and have a few beers with you.

Another great way to conserve fuel: put a brick in your petrol tank.

I asked Dad where babies came from. He said, 'Ask your wife!'

I take my pay to the bank every Friday – it's far too little to be going by itself.

Beware of the bloke who says he's in a stable relationship, he could be talking about horses.

My wife and I make love every single night. Of course, we hardly see each other anymore, but at least *she's* happy.

He's trying to give up half his sex life – but can't decide which half – the thinking about it or the talking about it.

Remember when 'safe sex' meant getting your pants back on before her parents got home?

He's a bilingual illiterate – can't read or write in two languages.

Left a sign in my car that said 'No mobile phone'. Came back, found the window smashed and a note that read 'Just checking'.

Dad was known as the town drunk. That doesn't sound too bad, but *Sydney's* town drunk?!

He was charged with sexual harassment in the workplace, which is very odd – he runs a one-man office.

I'm blind in one eye, but it's all right, I have double vision in the other.

I hate it when my missus refers to my erections as 'stand-up comedy'.

Ugly? She's so ugly we keep her photo on the mantelpiece to keep the kids away from the fire.

The difference between a poodle making love to your leg and a pit bull doing the same? The pit bull gets to finish!

He's such a dull speaker – the local animal shelter uses him to put unwanted pets to sleep.

If a patient dies in the bed next to you, it's perfectly OK to finish his two fruits and ice cream.

I think my wife learned all about sex at Our Lady of Perpetual Headaches.

Her first sexual experience was an assault, lucky the fellow didn't press charges.

Fat? He's so fat at the Easter Show one year he burned out two ferris wheels.

Failed Chinese sex therapist: Hung Bad Lee.

Talk about a dull movie, we had to leave a wake-up call with the usherette.

Remember, old actors never die – their parts just get smaller.

Accidentally hooked my VCR up to my microwave, watched *Gone with the Wind* in three minutes!

Remember, if you can't fill up the specimen bottle, simply pass it around the waiting room.

Remember chaps, as we get older, everything becomes harder – with one noticeable exception.

Remember that famous circus family, the flying Flabbertos, who were fired from cannons? Guiseppe Flabberto went crazy one night and started firing relatives into the crowd.

. . . He finally ended his own life with a loaded nephew.

Mobile phones are like arseholes, everyone's got one.

Opinions are like arseholes, everyone's got one but nobody is interested in yours.

As kids we used to walk a lot – mainly because Dad always forgot where he parked the car.

On her last visit to the beach, my wife almost drowned. The lifesaver was trying to give her mouth-to-mouth and she wouldn't stop talking.

Grandpa complained the Department of Social Security had him listed as deceased. They fixed it, they came around and shot him.

If you're in a hurry there's the Mexican jumping-bean salad – it tosses itself.

What about the bike for bisexuals? It's got a removable bar, depending on your mood.

If you cross an owl with an oyster, do you get a mussel that stays up all night?

Or if you cross a rooster with peanut butter, do you get a cock that sticks to the roof of your mouth?

As the elephant said to the naked man, 'Hey it's cute, but will it pick up peanuts?'

Ugly? He's so ugly that when he was born, his parents sued the hospital for not switching babies.

Weird? He's so weird he used to feed the pigeons in the park . . . intravenously!

Budget funerals: the widow gets to ride on the running board of the hearse.

My mate is so hard to buy for, what do you get the guy who's smoked everything?

Poor? As a child I was so poor I had to share my sandbox with the cat.

I'm such a cheapskate, when we visited Hollywood all we could afford was a tour of the extras' homes.

My ninety-year-old grandfather recently became a new father. It's great, he and the baby share the same nappy service.

It's such a posh church, for communion they give you a wine list.

My wife told me I'm a lousy lover. I said, 'How can you make a judgement like that in only ninety seconds?'

Terrible steak, you can still see the marks where the jockey hit it.

Fat? He's so fat he'd go to orgies just for the grapes!

Her plastic surgeon told her instead of having her nose reduced, it would be cheaper to have her face widened.

I was born under the sign 'Slippery When Wet'.

You've had too much to drink if your breath sets your pillow on fire.

It's me folks, the sex symbol for women who no longer care!

Attractive? She's so attractive she once got on a bus and five blokes offered her their seat – unfortunately, one was the bus driver!

Remember girls, there's no such thing as an ugly rich man.

My wife and I do the dishes as a team. I wash and she sweeps them up.

In Surfers Paradise, you're not legally dead until your tan fades.

Ugly? She's so ugly the cops found a Peeping Tom outside her window . . . asleep!

Your sex life is in trouble if your dog watches you to learn how to beg.

. . . Or if your wife uses you to time a soft-boiled egg.

A little-known symptom of shingles is the uncontrollable urge to nail yourself to a roof.

Another way to make your local member nervous: get his twenty-year-old secretary to call a press conference.

You know if you've been burgled if you come home and your dog is sitting where your telly and VCR used to be.

. . . Or if you get back from holidays and your next-door neighbour tells you the blokes in the moving van said to say 'Thanks!'

Ugly? He's so ugly he's got a job standing outside chemist shops making people sick.

Be careful if you walk into a bank and everyone is doing business face down on the floor.

. . . Or if you open your refrigerator and the bloke inside says the electricity company sent him around to change the light bulb.

My Uncle Frank visited Chernobyl last year. He now rents himself out as a night-light.

Skinny? She's so skinny when her chest gets sunburnt her back peels.

I have enough money to last me the rest of my life . . . provided I die before Christmas.

Little-known fact: 'Praise the Lord and pass the ammunition' was written during World War II by a soldier who had just swallowed a live hand grenade.

Bought a waterbed recently from Mafia Home Furnishings – there was this guy floating face down in it.

What goes in hard and pink and comes out soft and wet? Bubble gum (of course!).

Science has discovered that a speeding car can dramatically slow down the ageing process.

El Cheapo Airlines: they do crop-dusting on the way.

El Cheapo Funerals: for just one hundred dollars they put the deceased in the back seat of a car in a tow-away zone.

My girlfriend has the body of a jaguar . . . and the face of an FJ Holden.

He committed suicide by covering himself in Pal and throwing himself in front of a pit bull terrier.

Debate: it's what you use to catch de fish! *(ouch)*

The Catholic school I went to was so tough, Mother Superior was known as Attila the Nun.

Sure, I have property in Surfers Paradise. Actually, they just found my car stripped and abandoned up there.

He just majored in philosophy, he can't get a job but he does understand why.

The rhythm method song: everybody now! 'I've grown accustomed to your phase'.

When Dad retired, they didn't give him a watch. But they do call each day to tell him the time.

Let's not complain too much about the rain – in this country, it's about the only thing coming down.

He's such a heavy drinker mosquitoes bite him and then fly straight into a wall.

New Mafia restaurant opening specials: broken leg of lamb, crushed (prime) ribs and stuffed chicken (stuffed with another chicken).

At last, a more economical pacemaker. Just a few things to iron out though, like where to shovel the briquettes.

Today on TV: sex education for the elderly. Today's topic, what to do until the ambulance comes.

I'm off to the doctor straight away – if that was really a birthmark, it wouldn't be moving.

Yes, I am getting a little thin on top but I've found this great barber who gives braille haircuts.

What a night! When he woke up the next morning, found his clothes scattered all over the front lawn – problem was, he was still wearing them.

Girls, double your wardrobe. Marry a transvestite!

The neutron bomb evidently kills people but leaves buildings standing. A bit like your average home loan.

He went on one of those fad powdered-food diets – got caught in a rainstorm and exploded.

Remember kids, trial marriages are very dangerous – they *can* lead to the real thing.

Another question nobody's ever been able to answer: What makes teflon stick to the pan?

The difference between a wife and a mistress? A wife has real orgasms and fake jewellery.

Had sex with a real 'ten' last night. Of course on slow nights, she only charges five!

Fat? He's so fat when he talks about 'rolling his own' he's talking about rissoles.

Baptists never make love standing up – they're afraid God might think they're dancing.

Marriage means never having to leave money on the bedside table again.

I was going to stay in bed all day but the dog needed the kennel.

El Cheapo Airlines: the in-flight movie is the flight attendant's wedding video.

If you crossed a moose with a cow you'd have somewhere to hang your hat and coat when you milked it.

Another fad diet: eat all your meals in front of a mirror in the nude. Of course, some of our better restaurants will object, but . . .

The John Howard diet: only eat when he says something funny.

What a party! There she was, her head on my shoulder . . . someone else carrying her feet.

He's finally achieved physical compatibility with himself – his neck size and IQ are now the same.

I'm so hungover I think I drank something that made my tonsils grow back.

What do you call a woman who can suck a tennis ball through ten metres of garden hose? . . . Darling!

He loathes anything artificial in his coffee, even stirs it with his finger.

She told him she was fed up with the midnight feeding, the burping, the throwing up and the bed wetting – and they don't even have a baby.

Lonely? He's so lonely he spends most weekends teaching his inflatable girlfriend how to do the Pride of Erin.

Fat? He's so fat he bleeds internally just tying his shoelaces.

Graffiti: Apathy is a condition nobody cares about.

My friend's fat radar just started beeping – we must be near a McDonald's drive-thru.

Seen at a casino recently: famous Test bowler who during the craps game, thought it would bring him luck if he rubbed the dice on his groin.

I've never been back to that restaurant since I saw the chef putting Defender snail pellets around the salad bar.

My husband has such a bad snoring problem, each morning I have to get the kids to help me pull the bedroom curtains out of his nose.

Never drink alcohol in direct sunlight, it evaporates too quickly.

What do you get when you cross a TWA pilot with Carlotta? A transworldvestite.

Chap finds wife in bed with best friend. Says, 'I guess dinner isn't ready either?'

I have become the stranger my mother warned me about when I was a kid.

It's time to go on that diet if you have to smother yourself in baby oil just to get behind the wheel.

We had a very amicable parting – I got the divorce and she got everything else.

Bad driver? She's such a bad driver she's had more accidents than a woman using the rhythm method.

Talk about frigid in bed. Last night I threw the doona back and a little light came on.

Hey it's tough being the boss; having to decide where to do lunch each day.

He must have had a big night, his entire body is bloodshot.

Fat? He's so fat whenever he opens his mouth a little light comes on.

Ugly? She's so ugly when our T-bones arrived she took hers outside and buried it.

She had sixteen children, but young Kenny is still her favourite stretchmark.

Inexpensive beauty tip: use liquid paper to white out your varicose veins.

Grandpa always put women on a pedestal – just so he could look up their dresses.

It was so cold yesterday, our local flasher was just describing himself to women.

Ugly? She's so ugly she only wears high heels to stop her knuckles from dragging on the ground.

Hey kids, pornography can cause violence – especially when your mother finds it hidden under your bed!

My wife recently achieved a black belt . . . in shopping.

Vive la difference! When a bloke answers the phone, he reaches for a pen. When a woman does the same, she reaches for a chair.

Is ecclesiastic what a clergyman holds his underpants up with?

Another great way to stay awake whilst driving: stick your finger where the cigarette lighter goes!

Dracula: the original tax department training film.

Macho? He's so macho he can take an enema standing up.

He used to breed sheep . . . until he found out they could do it themselves.

If that bloke was any slower, he'd be in reverse.

He's about as much use as a lead parachute.

He's about as much use as a hip pocket in a singlet.

He's as popular as a tongue kiss at a family reunion.

He's as sharp as a bowling ball.

Definition of stupid: He's been swimming in the shallow end of the gene pool.

He's busier than a one-legged man in an arse-kicking contest.

He's as confused as a month-old baby in a topless bar.

He's got an inferiority complex – but he says it's not a very good one.

When there's nothing left to say, he's still saying it.

He started out with nothing, and he's got most of it left.

Talk about dull, he's got the personality of a snail on Valium.

She fell out of the ugly tree – hit every branch on the way down.

He's not a complete idiot, some parts are missing.

Talk about stupid, he's got enough sawdust between his ears to bed an elephant.

I wanted to marry into money – do you have any idea how few lady plumbers there are?

Ugly? She's so ugly her licence stipulates she can only drive after dark.

I was so drunk, I fell asleep as soon as my head hit the accelerator.

I asked the barmaid for a double – she brought a bloke out who looked just like me.

Loser? He's such a loser he used to go to the drive-in alone and do push ups in the back seat.

The Medical Institute of Dublin has just performed the first-ever successful separation of a Siamese cat.

Yet another thoughtful Mother's Day present: the ride-on vacuum cleaner.

Ugly? She's so ugly she has a special entrance at the local beauty salon marked 'Emergency'.

I gave up golf for sex. The scoring is easier and I don't have to change shoes.

Why are there so few female firefighters? Have you ever waited for a woman to get dressed?!

Our tax system is odd. You pay tax in 1998 on money you earned in 1997 . . . and spent in 1996!

Talk about a dead-end job. He's an eye-closer in a sardine factory.

Passionate? You can tell she's passionate by the way she digs her fingernails into your wallet.

This food tampering is getting serious, I actually found some meat in a pie the other day.

What happened to my beard you ask? I still have it but I keep it shaved off.

My wife holds garage sales just so she can meet other people with appalling taste.

When they made him they threw away the mould. Unfortunately it keeps growing back.

Fat? He's so fat he was last seen at the supermarket trying to put the frozen food section on lay-by.

He finally got rid of that tattoo on his leg. Actually, it got lost amongst his varicose veins.

Macho? He's so macho he jogged home from his vasectomy.

Talk about a dead-end job, he takes the knuckles out of fish fingers.

Ham sandwich walks into a bar and orders a beer. Barman says, 'Sorry mate, we don't serve food here.'

What do you get when you cross a pig with a centipede? Bacon and legs!

A vegetarian is someone who will not eat anything that can have babies.

'At least you could have let me off with a warning,' I said to the cop who booked me for speeding. He said, 'OK' and fired two shots over my head.

Windy? It was so windy I saw a chook lay the same egg three times.

Loser? He's such a loser he lost one hundred dollars at the casino last night . . . and that was just in the cigarette machine.

She was so nervous on our blind date – when I picked her up, she put the seatbelt around her knees.

Old? He's so old he's seen Halley's comet three times!

He's always looked old – even as a baby he had liver spots.

New Jewish locust: it destroys your crop but feels guilty about it afterwards.

I had such a deprived childhood, Dad ripped December 25 out of the calendar and told me I'd slept through it.

Graffiti: Stigmatism is in the eye of the beholder.

Budget tip: put all your bills into a shoebox each month – when it's full, move to another state.

I married a nurse. It's terrible, she wakes me up every two hours to ask if I'm comfortable.

My infant son and I have something in common – we both fall asleep after our bottle.

With my luck, if Dolly Parton was my mother, I'd be a bottle-fed baby.

Sexual attitudes have really changed. I know blokes who go to singles bars now just to get drunk!

We called her 'Doorknob', because everyone got a turn.

(One for the girls.) Why don't women have brains? They don't have a penis to store them in.

They had five sons and one turned out to be gay. Yes, he was the mauve sheep of the family!

He drives a BMW: a 'bent, mutilated wagon'.

Graffiti: Fame is fleeting – obscurity forever.

Immature? He's so immature, at his bucks night, he showed a *Flintstones* video.

At a lesbian wedding, who carries whom across the threshold?

. . . And the father of which bride pays for the reception?

The Irish hand grenade: it weighs 50 kilos.

She's so self-confident she does crossword puzzles in a typewriter.

Country and western song: 'I went home at two with a ten and woke up at ten with a two'.

Sex is like playing bridge – you don't need a partner if you've got a good hand.

Definition of stupid: Both oars are in the water, but on the same side of the boat.

Sure I know the primary colours, there's yellow, blue, Johnnie Walker red . . .

Woody Allen couldn't be with us tonight, he's had to rush off to hospital where he's awaiting the birth of his next wife.

To be honest about my public speaking experience, I've addressed more envelopes than groups.

Ugly? She's so ugly a Peeping Tom was arrested outside her bedroom window – his screams attracted the attention of the police.

He has no luck. Bought a rowing machine . . . it sank.

He's so well-endowed at our recent church picnic, he won the three-legged race all by himself.

. . . In fact he's known as the human tripod.

Whenever I went away camping with the scouts, Mum would sew name tags on my clothes. On my shirt it would say 'shirt', on my underpants it would say 'underpants' . . .

The doctor has got me on a bland diet of soups, custards . . . and Kenny G CDs.

Women! They can spot a blonde hair on your shoulder from ten metres away, but never see the car behind them when they're parking.

I couldn't afford a jacuzzi, so I put Alka-Seltzers down my underpants and jumped into the bath.

A tribe of cannibals was converted to Catholicism. Now they never eat fishermen on Fridays.

Windy? It was so windy the flashers had to keep bricks in their overcoat pockets.

The Australian Symphony Orchestra was banned from 'G' viewing time . . . Evidently too much sax and violins . . . *(Ouch!)*

When I was in the navy I was a frogman . . . and then my mates tried to get me interested in girls.

Repeating yourself is a sign of ignorance. If I've said that once, I've said it a thousand times.

I traced my family tree last week. Two dogs were using it.

Where the application form said 'Sign here' the blonde wrote 'Sagittarius'.

Inflation is catching up everywhere – the federal treasurer has just announced it now takes three to tango.

He's busier than a one-armed taxi driver with the crabs.

Grandpa's new pacemaker is a little faulty. Every time he gets an erection, the garage door opens.

Hernia: the Greek goddess of heavy objects.

Plato: the Greek god of false teeth.

How many gay guys does it take to change a light bulb? Two. One to call the electrician and one to mix the Martinis.

My wife wears curlers to bed . . . under her arms!

He could have been a top professional golfer. Unfortunately, at the age of twelve he was struck down by a tragic lack of ability.

He wanted to be a stand-up comic. He had the talent, had the gags, he just couldn't stand up.

He gave up being a stand-up comic. People kept laughing at him.

There was only one thing that kept him from being a major star . . . the public.

Time really flies . . . when you're under sedation.

My uncle lost all his money in a beef-breeding business. Bought one hundred head of cattle – ninety-nine bulls and one cow.

. . . Then he lost all his money in a poultry farm. Twenty thousand chooks and one gay rooster.

We were watching TV. 'God, this is boring,' she said. I said, 'If you think this is boring, wait till I turn it on!'

Talk about unlucky, Grandpa put his new set of teeth in a glass. Woke up the next morning, they were gone and the glass was full of twenty cent pieces.

Gentlemen, at a nudist colony funeral, it's perfectly acceptable to wear a black cigar band.

John Wayne Bobbit's favourite song: 'They Can't Take That Away From Me'.

Homer Simpson develops a drug and alcohol dependency. Marg books him into the cartoon ward of the Betty Ford clinic.

Got into an argument the other day with a handicapped bloke trying to use one of *our* toilets.

It's such a rich neighbourhood the local priest has stained-glass windows in his Mercedes.

Definition of stupid: He doesn't have his belt through all the loops.

My seatbelt has improved my driving – sitting on the buckle helps keep me awake.

My wife and I drove from Melbourne to Perth. We were very careful, took turns driving, swapped every five kilometres!

I get four weeks off each year . . . The two weeks when I go away and the two weeks the boss is away.

That speed-reading course did wonders – he can now finish a whole comic book in one night.

How come whenever I'm out driving, all the motorists waving at me don't use all their fingers?

My wife wanted to earn some extra money working around the house. It was going OK until the vice squad closed it down.

My wife was with me when I was sick, when I was broke, when the taxation department went through me . . . The bloody woman's a jinx!

His dentist took one look at his teeth and told him it would be cheaper to buy a dog to chew his food for him.

The C.S.I.R.O. tested my wife's cooking. The result: ninety-eight per cent of their laboratory rats have started bringing their own lunch.

Australia Post has brought out a new stamp featuring the Queen's corgis – it licks itself.

A consultant: someone who wears a hat when he craps so he knows which end to wipe.

We were so poor I had to wear hand-me-downs . . . and I only had an older sister.

. . . One day at school I had on the same dress as the teacher. I didn't care but *he* was really pissed off.

We use Vaseline as a sex aid – put it on the knob of the bedroom door to stop the kids getting in.

Fat? He was so fat when he died, the hearse had to make two trips.

He's pretty slow although he's getting better – he can now watch television without moving his lips.

She believed in natural childbirth – no lipstick or mascara.

The safest, cheapest form of birth control: no make-up and a hairnet.

He developed the world's first glow-in-the-dark bed pan. Unfortunately, the one hundred-watt globe made it a little too uncomfortable to use.

Loser? He was such a loser during World War II, he lent money to Kamikaze pilots.

My uncle drank a bottle of Scotch each morning after breakfast, smoked sixty cigarettes a day and made love to a different woman every night.
He died in his sleep on Monday . . . He would have been nineteen.

Great party! Would have got home sooner except people kept stepping on my hands.

One third of the world is ugly. Proof? Take a look at the person on your right then on your left. If they look OK, then you're the ugly bastard!

Great Britain has announced it will not be devaluing the pound – it will remain at sixteen ounces where it's always been.

A farmer got his marijuana mixed up with his superphosphate – his crops rotated themselves.

Premature ejaculation is hereditary . . . because it comes in your genes.

The new Mafia lollipop – a sucker dipped in cement.

Did you hear about the confused Royal Canadian Mountie who blew his horse and jumped on his whistle?

Screams coming from hospital ward: doctor to nurse, 'No, no you stupid girl, I told you to prick his *boil*!'

I have to hand it to my wife. Whenever she's right, she's the first to admit it.

A tree surgeon has just opened a branch in our suburb.

. . . Injured himself badly after falling out of one of his patients.

X-rated kids movie: *Benji Gets Lassie Into Trouble*.

Definition of stupid: His driveway doesn't quite reach the garage.

They're naming a street in Kings Cross after Fred Nile. It'll only go one way, though.

I was an only child – had to play hide-and-seek with myself.

Poor? I was so poor if I didn't wake up with an erection, I had nothing to play with for the rest of the day.

You know when you've had too much to drink when you try to take your pants off over your head.

Ugly? He was so ugly as a baby, his mum would feed him with a slingshot.

My wife's expert at removing spots from my pants – mainly ten spots and twenty spots.

A blonde got sacked from her job at the chemist. Kept breaking all the prescription bottles in the typewriter.

Can you believe it? Seven million sperm cells and *he* was the winner?

Waddya call a nun who's had a sex change? A transsister!

In their bedroom there are mirrors on all four walls and the ceiling. That way he gets a dozen different views of her headache.

What does a Jewish American princess say as she's about to orgasm? 'Mum, I've got to hang up now.'

Poor? My family was so poor as a kid, my first wind-up toy was a can opener.

Sure I have a passenger-side airbag – I married it twenty-five years ago!

He has such a dull sex life, he goes out to the airport and volunteers for full-body searches.

My wife prefers fiction to non-fiction . . . so I never tell her the truth.

In Heaven: the Poms are the police, the Germans are the engineers and the French are the cooks. In Hell: the Poms are the cooks, the French are the engineers and the Germans are the police.

She was only the rector's daughter, but you couldn't put anything pastor.

Fat? He's so fat he's tried diet foods – he likes them too.

Censorship ratings: 'G' nobody gets the girl, 'PG' good guy gets the girl, 'R' bad guy gets the girl, 'X' everyone gets the girl.

Another great way to slow cars down at school crossings: topless lollipop ladies.

She says she really likes being married, only not to me.

I never knew Grandma had tattoos, I always thought they were her *real* eyebrows.

In a gay suburb police recently broke up a riot with lemon-scented tear gas.

My wife's relatives are so ugly, when they sit out on the front lawn it looks more like Easter Island.

He has such a boring existence – each morning he goes through the death notices and then crosses their names out of the phone book.

My wife can recite the names of every Collingwood football club player. Unfortunately, she can only do this when we're making love.

Graffiti: One day obsolescence will be a thing of the past.

More graffiti: Old judges never die, they just stop trying.

The first person ever to put everything they owned on a horse? Lady Godiva of course!

Flew with Crashlandia Airways the other day. Their smoking section was the engine.

Fat? He's so fat they found a shadow on his chest X-ray. Luckily, it just turned out to be one of his chins.

Inflato: the Greek god of lonely men.

Korean version of Rolling Stones' hit: 'I'll Show You How to Wok the Dog'.

Isn't it interesting that once you pass your driver's licence test, you never drive like that again for the rest of your life?

A gift for people with plenty of spare time: a dictionary that's not in alphabetical order.

Our local hospital doesn't have a recovery ward because nobody ever makes it that far.

Sexual hygiene tip: never kiss anything that doesn't have lips.

My pet bird contracted an STD called chirpies. Although it's a canarial disease, my vet tells me it is tweetable.

She asked me to be gentle on our wedding night. So I didn't put any hotels on Mayfair or Park Lane.

Poor? We were so poor we had to put IOUs in the mousetraps.

The best thing about hospital food is that you don't have to go far to get your stomach pumped.

When I grow up I want to be a weather forecaster. Where else can you be wrong ninety-eight per cent of the time and actually get paid for it?

I'm a very tough act to follow, sometimes it can take them at least ten minutes to wake up the audience.

Definition of stupid: His lift doesn't go all the way to the top floor.

We have a great marriage – she goes her way . . . and I go her way.

Her parents were very strict. On our first date they made me take the back seat out of my car.

Another way to get unwanted guests to leave: turn your eyelids inside out.

He wasn't too successful at hunting crocs, we call him Crocodile Amputee.

Phoned home drunk one night. 'Where are you?' she said. 'At the corner of Walk and Don't Walk,' I said.

Election time: when each side accuses each other of doing what they wish they had thought of first.

The best way to find out a woman's real age is to ask someone who doesn't like her.

Of course he played a lot of football – he's got plenty of splinters from sitting on the interchange bench to prove it.

He's got about as much chance as a cat on the south-eastern freeway at peak hour.

He's so old he's been around since cocky was an egg.

You know you're past it when you keep hoping she'll say no.

I didn't get the rego number of the bloke who ran me over . . . But I'd know that laugh anywhere.

Fat? He's so fat whenever he walks backwards his hips go 'beep beep beep'.

I have three children. Two are living, one's in the public service.

The difference between a wedding vow and a poverty vow? Nothing!

When I was a teenager I was short and pudgy. Not any more though, now I'm bald as well.

I asked her if I was the first. She said, 'How come everyone always asks me that?'

Have you ever noticed old people always drive as though they're constantly looking for an address?

I told my shrink I thought I was a dog. Problem was he wouldn't let me up on the couch.

He delights in opening the car door for his wife, especially when they're doing one hundred kilometres an hour.

A pessimist looks at a bottle of Scotch and says it's half empty. An optimist says it's half full. I'm a realist, I look at the bloody thing and just drink it!

Always buy small cars – they make your house look bigger when you park out the front.

Did you hear about the leper who failed his driving test? Kept leaving his foot on the clutch.

Stupid? He's so stupid at school he was asked the capital of Victoria. He said 'V'.

Hey, I'm going to become a father in August – I just don't know how to tell my wife.

I'm not an only child – but Mum says if I'd been born first I *would* have been.

The government spends money like drunken sailors – but at least sailors spend their *own* money.

Definition of stupid: The boom gate's down, the lights are flashing, but the train ain't comin'.

Is Iran the past tense of Iraq?

Twenty-five years ago today I met the woman of my dreams. Unfortunately, it was one of the waitresses at our wedding breakfast.

Of course I'm in great shape. Each morning I do a twenty-minute work-out . . . followed very closely by a twenty-minute blackout!

Did you hear about the lepers' cricket game which was delayed for a while when someone dropped a ball in slips?

The best part about being the lead sled dog? The view!

Telstra cancelled my voice-mail service today – said my messages weren't important enough.

There was a very popular guy at the nudist camp – he could carry two cups of coffee and six chocolate donuts all at once.

My fat friend thinks chocolate is one of the major food groups.

We found out why our boy watches ten hours of television per day. When he grows up he wants to be a security guard.

Ugly? She's so ugly each morning she has to lie on a rock in the sun just to get her body temperature back up to normal.

He's tracing his roots. At the moment he's only got as far back as his Grandma's milkman.

I asked her what she wanted out of our marriage. She said, 'You!'

My wife's such a bad driver it only took her two and a half cars to get her licence.

I stopped doing that self-awareness course when I found out I really *was* stupid, short, fat and ugly.

I had such a deprived childhood my parents brought me home from the maternity hospital strapped to the roof-rack.

I worry when I find an empty plate in the fridge, makes me wonder if something else in there ate it!

The difference between kinky and perverted? Kinky uses a feather. Perverted uses the whole chicken.

Herpes: the Greek god of dance parties.

Ugly? She's so so ugly as a child she had all the normal childhood diseases: mange, rabies, distemper . . .

I've just consolidated all my debts. Now each month I have just one bill I can't pay.

Little-known fact: after making love, sharks relax by smoking a herring.

(Put down line just for you girls.)
Him: Hey, I'd like to get into your pants.
Her: Forget it, there's one arsehole in there already.

When I took her out to dinner, she ordered the most expensive things on the menu: a Big Mac and *large* french fries.

News flash: Marcel Marceau badly injured after falling down an imaginary flight of stairs.

Of course Elvis is alive, I just heard him singing on the radio.

I'm doing so much flying, I've joined the frequent survivor (drinker) program.

Grandma finally stopped Grandpa biting his nails – makes him wear shoes all the time.

His dad told him that generally it was boys on top and girls on the bottom. So when he got married he bought bunkbeds.

At the Mafia café there's a cover charge. When the shooting starts, they charge you for cover.

And now, from corn corner . . .

Thieves have just hijacked a truck containing two thousand kilograms of hair to be used in the manufacture of wigs. Police are combing the area.

A giant hole has appeared in the middle of High Street, authorities are looking into it.

All the toilets have been stolen from police headquarters. At this stage detectives have nothing to go on.

An incontinent elephant has had an unfortunate accident at the corner of High and Main Streets . . . Motorists are advised to treat it as a round-a-bout until the authorities clean it up.

. . . and now, we return you to our normal program

He's just like a Rubik's cube – square and very hard to understand.

And can anybody tell me what restaurants do with frogs' *arms*?

He wanted to donate his body to science, but his biology professor said she had other plans for the weekend.

So you like this suit? It was a surprise gift from my wife. Found it hanging over the chair in our bedroom when I got back early from a business trip.

Rhubarb: it's just celery with high blood pressure.

We were broken into by gay burglars – nothing stolen . . . they just rearranged the furniture.

My wife was set upon by a gang of gay muggers. Two of them held her down while one of them did her hair.

Today is the anniversary of the night I lost my virginity in the back seat of an FJ at the drive-in. I was nervous, I was sweating, I was fumbling . . . I was alone!

Ugly? She's so ugly the doctor told her to take two Pal Meaty Bites and call him in the morning.

He has such bad breath he can make yoghurt from milk just by breathing on it.

He got eighteen out of twenty for his driving test – two blokes managed to jump out of the way.

These days, when opportunity knocks, by the time you've looked through the peephole, tied up the Doberman, unlocked the deadlock and unhooked the security chain . . . It's gone.

He's so boring, once when he was drowning, John Howard's life flashed before his eyes.

Theirs was such an unhappy marriage – he fell asleep with a cigarette in his hand – and his wife lit it!

Fat? She was so fat we used to get her to sit in the back of the ute whenever we had to change a front tyre.

Count Dracula's favourite song: 'You're So Vein'.

My favourite Chinese bar: – 'Taiwan On'.

A night on the town with my heavy-drinking mate is a bit like writing music . . . Sixteen bars and a rest, sixteen bars and a rest . . .

I am so tired, the only thing holding me together is static electricity.

To lose weight, my overweight friend went to a fat farm – lost a quarter of an acre in the first week!

I never drink coffee at work – I toss and turn at my desk all day.

Fat? He's so fat convenience food to him is anything at the front of the refrigerator.

What do you call a dog with no legs? Nothing. He's not going to be able to come anyway.

At university I qualified as a B.A. – barely adequate.

I was an unwanted child. When I turned twenty-one, they gave me the key of somebody else's door.

The doctor said I'm not suffering from stress, but I am a carrier.

My teacher told me I would never amount to anything, but with my absentee record, I'd probably make a great prime minister.

Talk about a bad childhood, Dad used to take me on hunting trips with him – always gave me a three-minute start, though.

The doctor said to my mother, 'I don't like the look of your husband.' She replied, 'Me neither, but he works hard and he's nice to the kids.'

How many psychiatrists does it take to change a light bulb? Just the one. But the light bulb really must want to change.

How many Vietnam vets does it take to change a light bulb? You wouldn't bloody know mate 'cos you weren't there OK?!

Newsflash: Man attempting to walk around the world drowns off St Kilda pier . . . Details in our six o'clock bulletin.

I must be getting old – the candles now cost more than the cake.

What do you get when you cross a Venus flytrap with a forget-me-not? A plant that always remembers to do up its fly.

Short? He's so short whenever he's dancing he complains he never has anybody to talk to.

Our dog ate my dictionary last weekend . . . I've been feeding him castor oil but so far we haven't been able to get a word out of him.

Fat? He's so fat he can trace his family tree right back to Attila the Hungry.

Is a woman's sex change operation known as an 'addadichtomy'?

Ugly? She's so ugly she asked the waiter for a doggie bag and he put it over her head.

Nobody has ever found out how many sheep there are in New Zealand . . . Every time they try to count them, they fall asleep.

Payday is like the Logies at our house. Each week she says, 'May I have the envelope please?'

Graffiti: Old soldiers never die . . . Just their privates.

It's a scientific fact that seventy-five per cent of your body heat escapes through the top of your head. Which means you can ski naked if you're wearing a good hat.

What to say to someone in a gaudy outfit: Hey, nice suit. How many girls you got working?

We asked for the 'Chef's Surprise' . . . he mooned our table!

New on the market: an electric knife that runs on a.c. or d.c. We call it 'the gay blade'.

Our local newspaper is so boring, the dog falls asleep bringing it in.

Answer: Flood, earthquake, fire, divorce.
Question: Name four ways you can lose your house.

He/she is living proof that God has no quality control.

Fat? He's so fat he once went to a fancy dress party as A.F.L. park.

Just think, when they drop the big one, your answering service will be able to say, 'Hi, we're not in at the moment . . . but then again, neither are you'.

Nice coat. The last time I saw that much camel hair it had a hump and very bad breath.

Newsflash: Dole bludgers to strike for more money – they'll go back to work until their claims are met.

I must be getting old. I'm ready, willing and able, but not at the same time.

The two things in life you can enjoy without being good at: golf and sex.

We had a military wedding – well, put it this way, there were shotguns there.

Have you ever thought you actually might *be* what everyone's calling you?

If ever you're feeling unwanted or insignificant, try missing a couple of mortgage repayments.

One thing about working at a sex change clinic, you get to meet a lot of new women.

My poor mate as ID carries a letter of rejection from Diners Club.

I asked my alcoholic brother-in-law how long he could go without drinking. He said, 'About three blocks.'

He was such a loser – after his last meal on death row they made him wash his dishes.

Great new dance club for senior citizens: The Slipped Disco.

Grandma just got a thirty-two piece dinner set – her new teeth just arrived.

The federal government has finally found a way to shorten the dole queues. Everybody stands closer together.

Promiscuous? She was so promiscuous she failed her driving test six times. Just couldn't get used to the front seat.

Another girl failed her driving test ten times. Just couldn't get the hang of sitting *up* in a car.

. . . They both prefer tilting steering wheels. More head room.

Old? He's so old he's the only person I know with an autographed Bible.

Fat? He's so fat his tailor told him he couldn't let his trousers out any further . . . but he could install landing lights.

Arafat is *not* Arabian cellulite.

I think I saw *The Exorcist* about twenty times . . . I don't know what possessed me!

I never believed in the tooth fairy – until I saw the way my dentist walked.

Cash: the poor man's credit card.

Went to pray at Our Lady of Good Hands in Kings Cross . . . Turned out not to be a church!

The secret of a successful marriage, girls – keep your man happy, healthy . . . and home!

Transsexual's favourite song: 'I Want a Girl Just Like the Girl that Used to Be Dear Old Dad'.

Boring? He's so boring his favourite drink is a Harvey Wallflower.

What's the opposite of white? Blonde: 'Yolk!'

Fat? He's so fat his mother was in labour with him for so long, he was born under three star signs.

Stupid? He's so stupid on the job application form where it said 'phone number in case of emergency', he wrote '000'.

As Adam once said to Eve: 'Hey! I wear the plants in this family.'

Eve, the first woman ever to say: 'I haven't got anything to wear.'

Definition of popular: Any girl who can suck-start a Harley.

Remember, it doesn't matter how important you think you are, the size of your funeral is very dependent on the weather.

Stretch – the obscure and little talked about Marx brother.

Whenever the royal family have baked beans for supper, there's always a fight over who's next in line for the throne.

He married her to fill an empty spot in his life – the kitchen!

Talk about mean, he loves calling his mother on her birthday – can't wait to hear the catch in her voice as she accepts the reverse charges.

Remember, if at first you don't succeed, you're probably pretty bloody inadequate.

He was going to make a donation to the sperm bank, however nothing's firm yet.

I think all astrology is a load of absolute bulldust. But typically, we Cancerians can be pretty cynical.

My uncle opened a deli in Tel-Aviv. He's calling it Cheeses of Nazareth.

Hey kids! Just for fun, the next time you're late returning a book, tell the librarian *she* looks overdue.

During World War II the Japanese tried to brainwash my father but gave up during the spin cycle.

Pathetic excuse for a sickie: Sorry boss, I slept on my face all night and I'm too ugly to come in.

She loves a man in uniform – she's going steady with a deep-fryer at McDonald's.

I'm all for statues of our political leaders, gives the pigeons a chance to speak for us all.

I crossed my cat with a gorilla . . . now I get put out every night.

Definition of tragedy: A busload of lawyers plunging over a cliff . . . with three empty seats!

In Toorak (or Double Bay or other rich suburb), to qualify for the dole, you have to prove your Merc is over five years old.

They're putting a huge clock on the Leaning Tower of Pisa – they reckon if you've got the inclination, you ought to have the time.

Graffiti: Reality is a crutch for people who can't handle alcohol.

El Cheapo Airlines: no air-sickness bags, just wind-out windows.

A couple of great things about donating sperm: it's free and whoever heard of a jar with a headache?

She's such a nagger, if we were in the Garden of Eden, the figleaf would be going over her mouth.

My vet said my canary would sing better if I filed about five millimetres off his beak. I did that, he was dead by the time I got him out of the vice!

He's not fussy, to him, a 'ten' is anything with a pulse that walks upright.

Ugly? She's so ugly whenever she goes to the doctor, he calls in a vet for a second opinion.

Taxation office motto: It is better to give than to deceive.

Definition of fat: She's obviously living beyond her seams.

He walked into the party with a beautiful woman on each arm . . . which was really strange because he said he'd *never* get a tattoo.

In Toorak (or Double Bay or other rich suburb), handicapped parking is only for people who make less than one hundred and fifty thousand a year.

Definition of annoying: Just another peanut in the windpipe of life.

Fat? She's so fat whenever she goes to the beach she applies her blockout with a paintroller.

Definition of a status symbol: Whatever your neighbour has two of that you don't have *any* of.

Life is full of ups and downs, especially if you drink too much water before bed.

Told a dwarf a joke – went right over his head.

Not a good thing to say when picking a girl up for your first date: 'Wow Mrs Johnson, I can see where Debbie gets her tits from!'

Since marrying Soon Yi, Woody Allen has now become his own father-in-law.

Definition of an old gag: That joke is now officially old enough to vote.

As an immigrant, he arrived in this country unable to speak the language and with no skills – he knew even then he was destined for politics.

He's such a loser, had his name changed to 'Householder' so he would get mail once in a while.

Before that without *Reader's Digest* he didn't get any mail at all.

The local idiot is resting comfortably in hospital after surgeons removed a brain the size of a walnut from his tumour.

DNA: the initials of the National Dyslexics Association.

Dyslexic graffitist: There is no dog!

New South Wales graffiti: Sydney Sux . . . Auckland Seven.

Feminist graffiti: If he beats you, leave. What happens if he only comes second?

What's a blonde's favourite nursery rhyme? 'Hump Me, Dump Me'.

No man is an island but (insert well-known fatty's name) comes close.

Fat? He's so fat as a volunteer fireman, he'd put out fires just by sitting on them.

Graffiti: Life is like a Kleenex tissue – it's no good once you blow it.

It's comforting to know the chemicals in Bill Gates's body are worth no more than the ones in mine.

I was an unwanted child. My birth certificate is a letter of apology from a condom company.

. . . My parents used to measure my height by making a bullet hole on the wall just above my head.

Women write more graffiti in toilets because they have both hands free.

Traffic lights in a gay suburb: 'Mince' and 'Don't Mince'.

There is no truth in the rumour that virgin wool comes from very ugly sheep.

Loser? He's such a loser, he went to a singles bar the other night – the only thing he picked up was the bill.

If Joan of Arc was married, would her husband's favourite song be 'You Light Up My Wife'? *(Insert groan here)*

My teacher said I was illiterate. That's not true, my parents were married when I was born!

After years of research, an Irish university has finally successfully developed the artificial appendix.

A Frenchman's beret was blown into a cow paddock. He tried on six before he found the right one.

Seventy-eight per cent of the Earth is covered with water. The remaining twenty-two per cent is covered with mortgages.

Scientists have developed a chicken that can lay a ten kilogram egg – but just once!

My psychiatrist has two trays on his desk: one is labelled 'outgoing', the other 'inhibited'.

The best way to help the poor is not to be one of them.

Doctor: Well, first the good news. You're going to have a fatal disease named after you.

Simple arithmetic problem: Young Kenny has four marijuana joints. He smokes two. How many does he *think* he has left?

My wife and I now have separate bedrooms – I don't mind except she won't tell me where hers is.

Available now! The tupperware coffin – keeps you fresh for weeks just in case the doctors made a mistake.

My pit bull buried a bone yesterday – unfortunately it was still in the paperboy's leg.

Can't say I like ox tongue, I hate to taste something that might be tasting me.

At my no frills bank there are no security cameras, just a security guard who sketches everybody as they enter and leave.

What about the Jewish architect who wanted to cut the top off Sydney's Centrepoint Tower (or Melbourne's Art Centre spire or similar phallic edifice).

Talk about sadistic, he once nailed shut the door of a cuckoo clock.

Divorce only proves one thing: whose mother was right in the first place.

Johnnie: I know why my daddy's got such a big tummy.
Teacher: Why's that Johnnie?
Johnnie: 'Cos I saw mummy trying to blow it up last night!

He's been on the dole for so long, he's forgotten what kind of work he was out of.

Fat? He's so fat to him, a balanced diet is a Big Mac in each hand.

My dog only knows one trick – and he insists on doing it all over the house.

What's green, has six legs and if it fell out of a tree would probably kill you? A billiard table.

The difference between meat and fish? If you beat your fish, it dies.

Yet another lame excuse for being late: My dog forgot who I was and wouldn't let me out of the house.

Ugly? She's so ugly she could get a job testing flea collars.

If you want to be remembered and talked about forever, try forgetting your wife's birthday!

Bought his wife a toy poodle for their anniversary – she almost killed it putting the batteries in.

Ugly? She's so ugly when she walks into a bank, the security cameras throw themselves off the wall.

Now that I've won lotto, my daughter's getting that operation she's always wanted. She's been called 'sir' for the last time!

Definition of high cost of living: When you have to work like a dog to live like one.

He saw on telly that it takes just ten dollars a year to support a child in India, so he's sending his kid there.

After dinner last night at an expensive restaurant the feeling has only just started to come back in my wallet.

What do elephants and watches have in common? They both come in quartz.

Local circus announces the retirement of their human cannon ball. He was given a party, a gold watch and aimed at Surfers Paradise.

I just won a science-fiction award for my last book, '*Sex After Twenty-Five Years of Marriage*'.

Recipe for the Kim Beazley casserole: Step one – kill a herd of animals.

You know if you had too much to drink the night before if you wake up *inside* your waterbed.

You should never call a female dog a bitch until you've heard her side of the story.

My family was so poor if we smelled meat cooking, it was only because someone had set our dog on fire again.

Poverty is contagious: you either catch it from your kids (or your ex-wife!).

He's more fun than a gynaecologist with the hiccups.

I've discovered what's causing my tension headaches – keeping my rug on with a rubber band.

As the elephant said to the naked man, 'How the hell do you breathe through that thing!?'

Another question nobody's ever been able to answer: In a polygamous wedding, which bride gets carried over the threshold first?

I told my son about the birds and bees, now he wants to know what the bee is supposed to do when the flower's father walks in on them.

He just underwent a triple bypass – three girls told him to piss off!

I'm thinking of becoming a monk. I have all the qualifications: I have a bald patch, a brown bathrobe and haven't been to bed with a woman in over twelve months!

Went to a gay bar last night, rode the bucking machine side-saddle.

Have you heard that parable in the Bible about dole bludgers? You know, the multitude that loafs and fishes.

The magic hasn't gone out of their marriage – he still disappears every few weeks.

Rang a real estate agent in Sydney from a phone box and asked what I could rent for two hundred dollars a week. You're standing in it, he said.

I'm a real animal in bed – I sleep all through winter.

Latest diet: eat like a pig but hang out with someone who weighs two hundred kilos.

'I'm leaving all my money to the Salvos.'
'What about your wife?'
'Her too!'

Graffiti: Mimes discriminate against the blind.

When I die, I want to come back as Elle Macpherson's shower nozzle.

I got attacked last night by this bloke wielding a razor. Luckily, it wasn't plugged in.

From the misogynist's handbook: What's the difference between a dog and a fox? About four Bundy and Cokes!

At my old school gifted meant the few of us who could actually read.

Definition of bad form: When a person is choking in a restaurant and you ask him to nod if you can have some of his oysters.

I call my dog Herpes. He's a great dog, but won't heel!

What's six inches long and very hard? Goran Ivanisovich's surname!

After we got married we went back to the drive-in. Hey, guess what? They actually show movies there!

I asked our waitress for some condiments. She said they're in a machine in the men's toilet.

Ugly? She's so ugly she has a job out at the airport sniffing packages.

I told my wife we were overdrawn. 'No problem,' she said, 'I'll just write a cheque to cover it.'

The best part about marrying a fat person? Shade in summer, warmth in winter.

We went to a wine tasting and heard a critic talking about 'firm bodied, awful nose, shallow with a cheap bouquet'. He was talking about my wife!

One lesbian to another: Your face or mine?

I've joined Gamblers Anonymous, mainly because they open each day at twenty to one.

I was charged with indecent exposure but I got off – they couldn't see exhibit 'a'.

I was charged another time with indecent exposure and got off again. The evidence wouldn't stand up in court!

Why do rodeo riders make lousy lovers? They think staying up for eight seconds is a pretty good effort.

My wife bought me a fan for my birthday, he just sits there all day telling me how great I am.

Stingy? He's so stingy his idea of a night out is putting chairs on the verandah and watching TV through the window.

Met a mermaid with a great figure: forty-eight, twenty-five and seven dollars a kilo.

My mum used to suffer terrible morning sickness . . . everytime she looked in the basinet.

I'm just back from the frozen south. Actually I was visiting my ex-wife in Hobart.

Definition of plastic surgery: Putting your money where your mouth was.

I couldn't afford a holiday this year so I simply had myself paged at hotels in Port Douglas, Surfers Paradise and Noosa.

My dentist said he charged one hundred and fifty dollars for an impression, and then did a very bad Kamahl.

We have an open marriage: her mouth, my wallet.

Girls, if you can't afford a facelift, wear a tighter ponytail.

The best way to keep your kitty litter smelling clean and fresh? Get rid of the cat!

My Favourite Jokes

Mrs Goldbloom is playing in the shallows of Hamilton Island with her four-year-old grandson Aaron on a beautiful sunny day. Suddenly, the sky darkens and it starts raining. There's a clap of thunder, a bolt of lightning and a huge wave crashes onto the shore sweeping young Aaron out to sea. With dismay, she looks down at the spot where Aaron used to be then looks up into the heavens and wails, 'You call yourself a merciful God? I am an eighty-year-old woman, I have lived through two world wars and all sorts of tragedy and you choose to take the apple of my eye, my only grandson, Aaron . . . You call yourself a merciful God?'

With that, there is another clap of thunder, another bolt of lightning and yet another huge wave which crashes onto the beach depositing young Aaron unharmed and laughing, playing with his bucket and spade as though nothing had happened.

Mrs Goldbloom looks down at her grandson, looks up to the heavens, looks down again at Aaron, then, looking up to the sky says to God, 'He had a hat!'

Rough, tough stockman walks into a trendy inner-suburban pub with a crocodile, plonks it on the bar and says to the barman, 'I'll bet you a round of drinks for the house I can open this croc's jaws, stick my dick in his mouth, whack him over the head with a bottle and pull my dick out just before his jaws snap shut.'

'OK, you're on,' replies the barman.

The stockman duly performs his trick, hitting the croc over the head with a beer bottle and pulling his penis out just in the nick of time to the tumultuous applause of everybody in the bar.

Whilst the barman is serving drinks all round, the stockman says in a loud voice, 'Anybody else want to try it?'

'Yessss, I'll have a go!' says a little gay chappie from the back of the room. 'Just don't hit me over the head with the bottle.'

It's the annual meeting of the supernatural society and the convenor asks if anybody present has ever seen a ghost. Out of the thirty-five members, twenty hands go up. 'That's great. Now, how many members have actually touched a ghost?'

Fifteen hands go up.

'Hmmm, that's pretty impressive. Now, how many here have spoken to a ghost?'

Another twenty hands.

'OK, here's the big question. How many here have had sex with a ghost?' One little weasly bloke at the back of the room sticks his hand up.

'You've actually had sex with a ghost?' asks the convenor incredulously.

'Oh, a ghost?!' says the weasly guy. 'I'm sorry, I thought you said *goat*!'

Two New Zealanders are walking along a country road one afternoon and see a sheep with its head stuck in a fence. 'Gee, I wish that was Pamela Anderson,' says one.

'I just wish it was dark!' says the other.

Dave (looking at jar of rabbit droppings sitting on the table): 'Hey Dad, what's in the jar?'
Dad: 'Well son, they're called "smart pills".'

Dave: 'Can I try some?'

After throwing a couple into his mouth, Dave spits them out in disgust and splutters, 'These pills taste like rabbit shit!'

Dad: 'See son, you're getting smarter already!'

A bloke's in bed with a married woman when suddenly they hear a car pull up. 'Oh my God! It's your husband!' says the lover looking out the bedroom window. 'Where's your back door?'

'We haven't got one!' exclaims the wife.

'Where would you like one?' he replies.

The chief personnel officer of the CIA is interviewing likely candidates for the service. The first bloke, a twenty-four-year-old, sits down and the CPO asks, 'So Mr Parker, you want to join the CIA?'

'Yes sir, ah surely do sir,' blurts out the nervous potential recruit.

'Well son, to prove your worth to the CIA you must undergo a test of loyalty. In the next room is your wife. I want you to go in there with this gun and kill her.'

The young man disappears into the room, only to appear a few moments later, gun in hand. 'I'm sorry sir, we've only been married six months and I love her too much. I just couldn't do it,' he sobs.

'That's OK son, we completely understand. No hard feelings, I'm sure you'll find other work . . . Next!'

This time, it's a thirty-five-year-old bloke, married for ten years, who is put through the same ordeal with exactly the same result.

Enter the third candidate, a greying fifty-two-year-old bloke, married for thirty-two years. Accordingly, he is ordered into the room with the gun to prove his loyalty to the CIA. Five minutes goes past then all of a sudden all that can be heard are blood-curdling screams and much banging and thumping. Suddenly, the door is thrust open and there stands the fifty-two-year-old covered in blood, shirt torn and looking totally dishevelled.

'My God, man!' exclaims the CPO, 'what in God's name happened in there?'

'Well,' says the grey-haired candidate, 'you're not going to believe this but some dumb bastard loaded the gun with blanks so I had to beat her to death with the curtain rod!'

———————

Dockside during the Vietnam War. A troop ship carrying a load of young conscripts is about to depart for the war zone. Just as they pull in the gangplank, a young soldier rushes off the ship up to a nun standing nearby and says, 'Sister, I'm begging you, I don't want to go to Vietnam. May I hide under your habit until the ship sails?'

'Certainly my son. Under you go,' says the kindly nun.

As the ship pulls out from port, the young soldier emerges from beneath the habit and says with gratitude, 'Oh thank you, thank you sister. You've saved my life. But, I must confess, while I was under there, I looked up and saw your knickers.'

'That's nothing pal,' replies the nun, 'if you had've looked a bit higher you would have seen my *knackers* – I don't want to go to Vietnam either!'

———————

'Father, I have sinned. I allowed a boy to touch my breasts,' confesses young Kathleen.

'Hmmm, a mortal sin my girl,' says the priest. 'That'll be twenty Hail Marys and out into the fountain in the courtyard to splash your breasts with holy water . . . Next!'

'Father, I have sinned,' confesses young Mary, 'I allowed a boy to touch my fanny last night.'

'Hmmm, definitely a mortal sin my girl. That'll be thirty Hail Marys and out into the fountain to splash your fanny with holy water.'

As the two girls go about their punishment, young Rosie comes walking through the gates of the church and asks them what they're doing. After they tell her, she says, 'Well, would you mind keeping the water clean. It looks like I might be gargling it!'

———————

A bloke's in bed with a married woman when suddenly they hear the front door being opened. 'Oh my God,' she gasps, 'it's my husband! Quick, hide in the wardrobe!'

As he stands in the wardrobe, the bloke is startled to hear a small voice say, 'It's very dark in here.'

'Who the hell are you?' he asks.

'That's my mum you were bonking, mister,' says little Johnnie. 'And now I'm gunna scream.'

'Please don't,' pleads the man, 'your father will kill me.'

'OK,' replies Johnnie, 'but it's going to cost you money.'

'Oh all right,' says the lover, 'here's five dollars.'

'That's not enough, I'm going to scream,' says the little brat.

'OK, OK, here's twenty dollars!'

'Still not enough, I'm going to scream,' says the little voice.

'How about fifty dollars then?'

Little Johnnie replies, 'Make it a hundred and you've got a deal.'

Feeling quite relieved, he hands over the hundred, the husband finally leaves and the lover beats a hasty retreat.

Later that afternoon, the little boy's mother takes him shopping and, as they're walking past a video game shop, he says, 'Hey Mum, I want that Nintendo game.'

The boy's mother says, 'No you can't have it, it's too expensive.'

'But I've got a hundred dollars!' boasts young Johnnie.

The mother asks, 'Where did you get that from? Did you steal it?'

Naturally, the boy doesn't talk. His mother persists and starts berating him even more severely to the point where she slaps his face. Still he doesn't 'fess up. Finally, twisting his arm, she drags him into a nearby church and approaches the parish priest. 'Father, my son has one hundred dollars and won't tell me where he got it. Perhaps you could find out.'

The priest nods and leads the boy into the confessional booth. The boy sits on one side and the priest on the other. The boy says, 'It's very dark in here . . .'

'Now don't start that again!' the priest replies.

An ancient old codger shuffles into a brothel and says to the receptionist, 'I'd like a girl for a couple of hours.'

The receptionist asks, 'Oh yeah, so how old are you?'

'Ninety-five,' he says proudly.

'Piss off pop, you've had it!' the receptionist replies.

'Oh really?' the old bloke says, fumbling for his wallet. 'How much do I owe you?'

———

A four-year-old wanders up and down the aisles of a supermarket crying his eyes out. 'What's the matter young fella?' asks a concerned shop assistant.

'I've lost my mummy!' wails the youngster, sobbing convulsively.

'Don't worry, we'll soon find her,' soothes the shop assistant. 'Now, what's mummy like?'

'Big cocks and vodka,' sobs the little fella.

———

The scene: an exclusive restaurant where a wine wanker, sitting with a group of ten friends, is boasting he can identify any wine blindfolded. A dinner napkin is produced and his eyes are covered. One by one, glasses of wine are duly handed to him for tasting. 'Lafite-Rothschild 1958,' he declares, followed by 'Bernkasteler badstube, 1951!' Infuriatingly, he is always right.

Finally someone hands him one he can't identify. After taking a sip, he spits it out, and, ripping off the blindfold splutters furiously, 'This is fresh urine. Plain, fresh urine!'

And a little cynical voice at the end of the table is heard to say, 'Yeah smartarse, but *whose*?'

———

Two blokes are discussing their latest exploits. George says to Harry, 'Yeah, I've taken up skydiving – it's really great. First they teach you how to fold your parachute and then we practise when to pull the ripcord and what to do in an emergency. We went up in a plane for the first time last week.'

'Wow! So how did it go, were you scared?' asks Harry.

'I'll say!' says George. 'There we were, all twelve of us at fifteen thousand feet, jumping in groups of four. I was in the first group, but just as we were about to dive out the door, I lost my nerve and said to our instructor maybe I should go in the next group. Anyhow, the next group gets ready to jump and, bugger me if I don't start crapping myself yet again and ask if I can go with the last group. Anyhow, just as they're ready to go, I really freak out and tell the instructor I just can't do it.'

'What'd he say?'

'Well, he reaches behind the bulkhead and pulls out this broomhandle and says to me, "George, I've been training you for six months in the lead up to today and, if you don't jump, you know where I'm going stick this broom handle don't you?"'

'So, did you jump?'

'Yeah, a little bit at first.'

Mother takes daughter to doctor concerned about strange symptoms. On examination, the doctor says, 'I'm afraid your daughter's pregnant Mrs Jones.'

Shocked and amazed, Mrs Jones replies, 'That's impossible! My daughter has had absolutely nothing whatsoever to do with men, have you dear?'

'That's right Mummy, I've never so much as kissed a man.'

The doctor looks from mother to daughter and back again then silently stands up and walks over to the window. He stares out for quite some time saying nothing until the mother feels compelled to ask, 'Doctor, is there something wrong out there?'

'No Mrs Jones,' he replies, 'it's just the last time something like this happened, a star appeared in the east and I'm just looking to see if another one was on its way.'

'So,' says the teacher to her class of eleven-year-olds, 'there are three crows sitting on a fence, the farmer shoots one of them, how many are left?'

'Please Miss!' shouts little Johnnie thrusting his hand in the air, 'I know, I know!'

'Yes Johnnie, how many crows do you think are left?'

'None Miss.'

'No, that's wrong – there would be two crows left. How did you arrive at none?'

'Very simple Miss. You see, when the farmer shoots one crow, the others would fly away in fright,' says Johnnie.

'Well, that's not exactly the answer I was looking for, but I *do* like the way you're thinking,' says the teacher.

'In that case Miss, I have a conundrum for you. There are three ladies sitting at a bus stop eating ice creams. One's licking her ice-cream, one's biting her ice-cream and one's sucking her ice-cream. Which one's the married lady?' asks little Johnnie.

After some thought, the teacher replies somewhat warily, 'Errr, the lady *sucking* the ice cream?'

'No Miss, the lady with the wedding ring. But I like the way *you're* thinking!' says Johnnie.

It's late Friday afternoon and Ken's boss tells him he has to work overtime to get an urgent order out. Ken and his wife have just shifted into a new house and the phone's not on yet so there is no way Ken can let his wife know he'll be late home. 'That's OK,' says the boss, 'it's on my way home, I'll stop by and tell her myself.'

On arrival at Ken's house, the boss is greeted at the door by the wife who is dressed seductively in a see-through nightie. 'I'm Ken's boss and I've called around to tell you he won't be home until late,' he says, '. . . and I would like to make mad, passionate love to you right now.'

'How dare you!' says Ken's wife, flushed with rage.

'What if I offer you one hundred dollars?' says the boss.

'Absolutely not! What a nerve you have . . .'

'OK, how about two hundred then?'

'Er no . . . I mean what kind of a woman do you think I am?' she says, slowly weakening.

'OK, three hundred and that's my last offer,' says Ken's boss.

'Oh all right, let's go upstairs and do some business,' she says finally relenting.

After making mad, passionate love for an hour or so, the boss departs, leaving three hundred dollars on the bedside table.

Later that night, Ken arrives home and, sneaking into the bedroom, trips over the cat, waking his wife. 'Sorry to wake you dear. Did the boss call in to tell you I'd be working late?'

'Why yes he did,' says his wife.

Ken spies the money on the bedside table and says, 'Ah good, I see he brought that three hundred he owed me as well.'

A man arrives home to find his best friend in bed with his wife. 'Hey! What in the bloody hell do you think you're doing?' he exclaims.

'See,' says his wife to the bloke in bed beside her, 'I told you he was stupid.'

An elderly couple – he's ninety-five and she's ninety-four – walk into a lawyer's office. The old gentleman says in a quavering voice, 'Gertrude and I want a divorce.'

'A divorce?' asks the lawyer. 'But why have you left it till now to get a divorce?'

'We thought it best to wait until all the children had died,' says Gertrude.

An old Irishman is lying on his deathbed, his son by his side. Paddy knows his time is near and leans over and whispers in his son's ear, 'Liam, I want you to go for the Protestant minister.'

'Dad! A Protestant minister? You were raised a good Catholic, you brought all us kids up to be good Catholics, what in the world would ye be wantin' with a Protestant minister at a time like this? It's the priest you'll be wantin' to be sure!' exclaims the dismayed Liam.

'Just do as you're told, me boy. If you respect your father, you'll grant him his last wish. Now, go fetch the minister,' orders Paddy.

Liam relents and brings the minister who duly converts Paddy to a Protestant.

About one hour later, Father O'Flaherty arrives and Liam says, 'I'm afraid you're too late Father – he's a Protestant now.'

Father O'Flaherty runs up the stairs and bursts into the bedroom. 'Paddy, Paddy, why did ye do it?' he cries. 'You were raised a good Catholic, we went to Saint Gregory's together, you were there when I performed my first Mass! Why in God's name would you do such a thing at a time like this?'

'Well,' says old Paddy, 'I figured if somebody had to go, it was better one of *them* than one of us.'

———

Young couple on their wedding night getting undressed: he throws his trousers at her and says, 'Here put these on.'

'What for?' asks the bride.

'Never mind,' says the husband, 'just put them on.'

She puts them on and even after fastening the belt to the last notch, they keep falling down around her ankles. 'I can't wear these,' she says.

'That's right,' our little chauvinist friend says, 'that's just to remind you who wears the pants in this marriage.'

With that, the bride takes off her panties and tosses them over to the husband. 'Here, you put these on then,' she says.

'But why?' he protests.

'You made me do it and it's only fair that I have equal rights – put them on,' she orders.

Reluctantly, and with great difficulty, the husband attempts to put on the panties but they're much too small. In fact he can't even get them up past his thighs. 'I can't get into these,' he says.

'That's right,' she says, 'and you're not going to until you change your attitude my man.'

———

Weedy looking bloke walking along a beach one hot afternoon comes across a bevy of beautiful, bikini-clad girls all admiring a sun-tanned adonis. They're all laughing at his every word and paying him a lot of attention. Eventually he leaves with a couple of them for what is obviously going to be a wild afternoon of passionate love-making.

The next day, the weedy bloke sees the same guy laying down his towel on the beach. Curious as to how he attracts so many beautiful women, he approaches him and says, 'Hey mate, I saw you here yesterday with all those beautiful sheilas. What's your secret?'

'Well, I'll tell you,' says the Greek god. 'What you do is put a potato down your swimming trunks. Drives the birds mad.'

'Wow!' thinks the weedy guy. 'I'll try that a bit further down the beach and let you know how I get on.'

About one hour later, the weedy guy comes up to the adonis and says to him, 'Hey Spiros, that trick you taught me doesn't work. Every sheila I tried chatting up started screaming and ran away.'

'Did you put the potato down your trunks like I told you?' asks Spiros.

'Yeah, of course I did. Look!' says the dweeby guy.

'Bloody idiot! You're supposed to put the potato down the *front*!'

———

Bloke's in bed with a woman. Suddenly they hear a key in the lock. 'Quick it's my husband,' cries the woman. 'Jump out the window!'

Totally naked, he jumps out of the window, right into the middle of the annual 'City to Surf' marathon. Acting as nonchalantly as he can, he falls into step with all the other runners. A surprised jogger running next to him says, 'Hey mate, do you always run naked?'

'Yep,' says the bloke, as he keeps jogging along.

'OK, tell me this then,' says the fellow runner, 'do you always wear a condom when you run?'

'Only,' puffs the naked bloke, 'if it looks like rain!'

———

Father O'Leary and his good friend, Rabbi Leibowitz, are playing golf together one day. As they're walking down a fairway, the priest says to the rabbi, 'Sol, we've been friends for many years. Do you mind if ask you a very personal question?'

'Why no,' says the priest's best friend.

'Have you ever eaten pork?' asks Father O'Leary.

'Well yes, I did once eat some pork,' admits the rabbi. 'But you tell me this – have you ever made love to a woman?'

'As a matter of fact I have,' replies the rather embarrassed priest.

The rabbi leans a little closer to the priest and says in a whispered tone, 'Sure beats the taste of pork eh Michael?'

———

The phone rings. Bloke picks it up – it's his doctor. 'Hi doc, have the results of my tests come through yet?' he asks.

'Well, yes they have and I'm afraid I've some bad news and some even worse news for you Mr Smith,' says the doctor.

'Well, you'd better hit me with the bad news first then doc,' says the bloke.

'I'm sorry Mr Smith, but you've only got twenty-four hours to live,' says the doctor.

'Christ! Well what's the even *worse* news, then?'

'I've been trying to ring you since yesterday!'

———

This story is supposedly true: A young lady being interviewed on a dating game show was asked a series of questions about her experiences with past dates. 'And tell me this, Charlene,' asked the host, 'where's the most unusual place you've ever made love.'

'Ummm . . . in the bottom I think,' she replied innocently.

———

Bloke running late to pick up some racehorses from Flemington is pulled over for speeding in Racecourse Road.

Cop comes up to the window of his car and says, 'Now tell me sir, what's your reason for doing eighty kilometres an hour in a built-up zone?'

'Well you see, officer, I've got a couple of horses in the float and I've gotta get them to the course in time for the next race,' explains the hapless driver.

'I see,' says the cop. 'Then you won't mind if I take a look in the back then?'

A few seconds later, a very angry cop is back at the window of the car and says, 'I can't see any horses in that float.'

'Don't tell me they've given me the bloody scratchings again!' replies the driver.

Three fellas are discussing their sex life together for the first time over a few beers after playing golf. One says, 'Me and my missus have been married for twenty years and probably make love at least once a week. How about you?' He asks the second chap.

'Well, we've only been married for a year and we seem to be doing it every day,' says the young bloke. 'And what about you?' he says, turning to the rather shy, middle-aged third player.

'Hmm, let's see,' he says. 'Last year I think it was about four times.'

'Four times!' they laugh, 'what sort of a sex life is that?'

'Well it's not too bad for a Catholic priest with a very small parish,' he replies.

The wife could not get her lazy, layabout husband to do any repairs around the house. He'd just sit there day after day in front of the telly, not budging an inch. Whenever she'd ask him to replace a tap washer he'd say, 'Do I look like Mr Plumber?' If she wanted her vacuum cleaner fixed he'd say, 'What do I look like, Mr Electrician?' Or if she wanted the lawns mown, he'd say, 'What do I look like, Jim's Mowing?'

Finally, she'd had enough. The next morning she phoned the plumber, the electrician and the gardener to come and fix all the problems. When her husband got home and she told him everything had been fixed he frowned and said, 'How much is all that going to cost?'

'Well darling,' she answered, 'they all said I could pay them by baking a cake or having sex with them.'

'Well, what kind of cakes did you bake them?' he asked.

She smiled at him and said, 'What do I look like? Sarah Lee?'

Behavioural scientists have discovered there are four kinds of sex that most men will have in a lifetime. Firstly there's 'house sex'. That's the sex you have in any and every room of the house when you first get married.

Next is 'bedroom sex'. That's the sex you have strictly in the bedroom after about five years of marriage.

Then comes 'hall sex' – after you've been married for over twenty years, you pass each other in the hallway and say, 'Screw you!'

And finally there's 'court room sex'. That's where your wife and your lawyer screw you in the divorce court for every cent you've got in front of a lot of strangers.

A man and his wife attending a country air show see the owner of a tiger moth standing in front of his plane. 'How much for a joy-flight?' asks the husband.

'Forty dollars for ten minutes,' replies the pilot.

'Geez, that's a bit expensive. Forget it,' says the husband.

'Tell you what,' says the pilot, not wanting to lose a fee, 'I'll do a deal. If you and your wife don't say a word during the flight, the joy-flight's free. But, if either of you utter a sound, I'll charge double.'

The couple agree and the pilot takes them on one of the most hair-raising joy-flights they've ever been on.

On landing, the pilot says to the husband, 'I must congratulate you for not making a sound. You certainly are a very brave man.'

'Thanks mate,' says the husband, 'but I've gotta tell you, I almost screamed when the missus fell out.'

A magician is working his passage on a cruise ship performing nightly in the cabaret show. His speciality is sleight-of-hand card tricks. Each night however, his performance is ruined by the ship's parrot who hops from table to table squawking, 'Raark raark! It's up his sleeve, it's up his sleeve . . . it's in his pocket, it's in his pocket . . . it's in his mouth, it's in his mouth! Raark raark!'

The magician, exasperated by the parrot, finally grabs the little feathered pest and threatens to kill him if he ruins his act one more time.

That night, just as his act is reaching a finale, the ship hits an iceberg and sinks within seconds – the magician and the parrot the only survivors, bobbing around the ocean in a liferaft. Regaining consciousness, the magician awakes to find the parrot sitting on the bow fixing him with a beady gaze. After a couple of hours just staring at him, the parrot eventually says, 'OK, I give up. What did you do with the bloody ship?'

A duck walks into a pub and says to the bartender, 'Can I have a beer?'

The barman replies, 'Nick off, we don't serve ducks in here!'

The duck waddles out, only to return the next day. 'Can I have a beer?' asks the duck.

'I told you yesterday and I'll tell you again today – we don't serve ducks in this hotel. Now, if I see you in this hotel again, I'll nail your stupid beak shut,' yells the barman.

The duck comes back the very next day and says, 'Hey barman, have you got any nails?'

The bartender says, 'No.'

'Good. I'll have a beer then!' replies the duck.

The Pope is on a visit to New York. After a hard day in the Popemobile, he is being chauffeured back to his hotel in the back of a stretch Mercedes. Having never driven one before, he begs the driver to let him have a go.

Reluctantly, the driver agrees and the Pope, not being used to such a high-powered car, soon finds himself travelling way over the speed limit. Of course, it's only a matter of time before he's pulled over by a cop car. The cop takes a look in the back and then in the front and radios back to the police station that he's just pulled over someone very, very important.

His superior officer asks him, 'Who? A movie star? The president? A prime minister? Who?'

'I don't really know, sir,' stammers the cop, 'but he must be pretty goddamn important – the Pope's his chauffeur!'

Young Jewish kid is not doing very well at maths at a Jewish school. His very worried father decides to send him to a Catholic school because he hears they're pretty good when it comes to this particular subject. At the end of his very first term, young Jacob's report card reads Bs and Cs in most subjects but straight As in maths. His dad is as pleased as he is mystified and asks his son how he came to do so well in maths at last.

'Well Dad,' replies Jacob, 'I really knew those micks meant business when I walked into the classroom and saw the guy they had nailed to a plus sign!'

A salesman driving along a lonely country road late at night sees a sign 'Sisters of Mercy House of Ill Repute – twenty kilometres.' A bit further along, he comes across another sign, 'Ten kilometres to the Sisters of Mercy House of Ill Repute.' By this time, his curiosity is getting the better of him and when he sees yet another sign, 'Sisters of Mercy House of Ill Repute – next right,' he follows it.

Pulling in to the courtyard, he climbs the steps and knocks on the huge wooden door which is opened by a nun dressed in the traditional long, black habit. 'Yes, my son?' she says in an ecclesiastical tone.

'Uh, er, hi sister. I noticed your signs coming down the road and thought we could do some business,' stammers the nervous salesman.

'Why of course, my son – walk this way,' says the kindly nun.

He is led through many dark winding passages and pretty soon becomes totally disorientated. Finally, the nun says to him, 'Please knock on this door.'

The door is answered by a very attractive nun holding a tin cup who instructs him to place one hundred dollars in it – which he dutifully does. He is then instructed by that nun to go through the large wooden door at the end of the corridor. Eagerly, he runs to the door, opens it and goes through it.

Suddenly, it's slammed shut and bolted behind him and he finds himself back outside in the car park. Totally confused, he looks around and then sees a sign that says 'You have just been screwed by the Sisters of Mercy'.

Teacher says to classroom of eleven-year-olds, 'I want you to give me a sentence with the word "lovely" in it twice.'

Little Mary stands up and says, 'Please Miss, yesterday Mummy took me into town – we had a lovely tram ride and went into Myer and bought some lovely things.'

'Very good Mary,' says the teacher. 'Yes Kathleen, I think you had your hand up next. Can you give me a sentence with the word "lovely" in it twice?'

'Yes Miss. This morning when I got up, I was greeted by a lovely sunrise and then I had a lovely breakfast.'

'Excellent!' says the teacher as she notices little Hamish down the back vigorously thrusting his hand in the air. 'Yes Hamish, you're the last – what's your sentence with "lovely" in it twice?'

'Well Miss, last night my sister told Dad that she was pregnant and didn't know who the father was and he said, "Lovely – that's just bloody lovely!"'

Murphy, the first-ever Irish astronaut, is on a mission to the Moon. With him on the flight is a monkey. Just before they're loaded on board the rocket, the flight commander gives each an envelope containing instructions for when they land. Finally the big day comes, the rocket is launched and they land on the Moon. The monkey opens his instructions which read, 'Unpack special robotic arm, assemble remotely controlled lunar vehicle. Deploy vehicle across lunar surface and collect three different kinds of mineral samples. Identify and label each sample and place in special airtight container for transportation back to Earth'.

Murphy then opens his envelope which reads: 'Feed the monkey'.

A tycoon arrives home from a long meeting with his accountant. 'How did the meeting go?' asks his wife as she prepares him a Martini.

'Not good. He says we're down to our last million and, if we don't pull our belts in, he says we'll be broke by Christmas.'

'What are we going to do then?' asks his wife.

'Well, if you could bloody well cook, we could get rid of the chef,' says the husband.

'In that case,' says the wife, 'if you were a bit better in bed, we could sack the chauffeur!'

Teacher asks her class of third-graders one morning what their fathers do for a living.

'Please Miss, my father works in a bank,' says young Sarah.

'Very good,' says the teacher. 'Yes Kylie?'

'My dad's a carpenter, Miss.'

'Excellent! Yes Bernadette?'

'Yes Miss, my father's a policeman,' she says.

'Thank you Bernadette. And you Johnnie?'

'Please Miss, my father's a piano player in a brothel, Miss.'

Somewhat aghast, the teacher dismisses the class for lunch and heads straight to the office where she rings Johnnie's father. 'What's this your son tells me about you being a piano player in a brothel?' she demands.

'Oh,' says the father, 'actually, I'm a lawyer but you can't tell *that* to an eight-year-old.'

(A golden oldie.) A young bloke decided to buy his girlfriend a gift for her birthday whilst he was holidaying interstate. As they hadn't been going out for very long, he decided that perhaps a pair of gloves would be a safe bet – romantic, but not too personal.

Accompanied by his sister, he went into David Jones and bought a pair of gloves; his younger sister purchasing a pair of lace panties for herself. Unfortunately, during the wrapping, the sales assistant mixed up the items – the sister getting the gloves and the boyfriend getting the panties. Without checking, he sealed the package and mailed it to his sweetheart with the following note:

Dearest Sharon,

I chose these because I notice you never wear any when we go out of a night. I'm glad my sister was with me when I bought them otherwise I would have chosen the long ones with buttons, but she says she wears short ones that are easy to get off.

You will note these are a delicate shade, but not to worry, the shop assistant showed me a pair she'd been wearing for the past four weeks and they were barely soiled.

I just wish I could be there to put them on you for the first time as, no doubt, many other hands will come in contact with them before I have a chance to see you again.

A little advice: when you take them off, it's always wise to blow in them before putting them away, as they will probably be a little damp from wearing. Another little trick is to sprinkle some talcum powder in them – this makes them a little easier to slip on if you're in a hurry.

I can't wait to kiss them when I next see you and trust you'll be wearing them when I get off the plane on Friday.

All my love,
Bobby

P.S. I believe the latest fad is to wear them folded down with a little fur showing.

Elderly Jewish lady is walking through a park one sunny afternoon when all of a sudden a pervert jumps out from behind a tree and opens his overcoat flashing his landing gear at her. She looks at him in disgust and says, 'Lining? You call that lining?'

Same Jewish lady. Later that night the phone rings. 'Hullo?' she says. On the other end a pervert proceeds to go into graphic detail of how he's going to come around and do unspeakable sexual things to her body. After five minutes, he's finally finished, to which she replies, 'I get all of this from just one "Hullo"?'

A young Italian boy and a young Jewish boy are good friends and both come of age on the same date. The Italian boy's father presents him with a brand-new pistol, whilst for his bar mitzvah, the Jewish kid gets a magnificent gold watch.

The next day at school, whilst comparing gifts, they decide that they like each other's present better so decide to swap. When the Italian kid gets home his father sees him playing with the watch, and asks, 'Hey Luigi, where did you getta the watch?'

Luigi explains and his father goes ballistic. 'Are you crazy? You bloody stupid boy – whatsamatter you?' he yells.

'Why are you so angry Papa?' asks Luigi.

'I tella you why! Somma day, you maybe gunna getta married. And somma day maybe you gunna come home and catcha your wife in bed with another man. Waddya gunna do? Look atta your watch and say, "How longa you gunna be?"'

A woman's playing golf with her husband when she's struck by an errant golf ball just after starting her round. Panic-stricken, her husband rushes back to the clubhouse to get help. 'Where was she struck?' asks the manager.

'Between the first and second hole,' replies the husband.

'Hmmm,' says the manager, 'that's a very difficult area to bandage.'

A priest has been called urgently to the house of one of his flock . . . It seems Murphy is dead. As he rushes through the door, he sees Mrs Murphy. 'Mrs Murphy, I'm sorry I couldn't get here quicker. Please, I must know, what were your husband's last words? It's very important.'

Mrs Murphy ponders the question for a minute and says, 'Oh yes Father, I remember, I think he said, "For God's sake Mary, put that gun down!"'

At the local prison, there's a problem with their electric chair. The governor calls Murphy's Electrical Repairs: no job too small to come out and see what's wrong.

Murphy duly arrives and the governor shows him to the execution room. 'See what you can do Mr Murphy, we do have an execution tomorrow,' says the governor.

'Leave it to me,' says Murphy, 'I'll have this thing fixed in a jiffy.'

Four hours pass and the governor becomes a little concerned. He sticks his head inside the execution room and there's Murphy with the electric chair in hundreds of pieces all over the floor. 'Well?' asks the governor, 'have you found the problem?'

'Oh, indeed I have sir,' says Murphy, 'and just in the nick of time, too. This thing was a real death trap!'

A troubled young man tells his psychiatrist, 'Doc, I've just started work in a pickle factory and I've been overcome by a tremendous urge each day to stick my penis in the pickle slicer. Is this unusual? I'm very worried.'

'Not really,' says the doctor, 'I once had a patient who had an obsessive urge to put his hand on a red-hot iron.'

'And did he do it?' asks the young man.

'Why yes he did,' says the doctor, 'and not only did he burn himself badly but he never had the urge again. So my advice to you would be: if you have an urge to stick your penis in the pickle slicer, follow your impulse and try it.'

The young man comes back for his next consultation and the doctor asks him if he followed his advice. 'Yep, I sure did, doc,' says the young man. 'I stuck my penis in the pickle slicer.'

'And what happened?' asks the doctor.

'Well,' replies the young bloke, 'they gave us both the sack!'

A man is about to cross the road when he's stopped by a passing funeral procession. Just behind the hearse is a chap with a Doberman straining at his leash and a long line of men right behind them. Overcome with curiosity, the bloke catches up to the fellow with the dog and asks, 'Excuse me, I'm sorry to trouble you at this time of grief but I've never seen such a long funeral procession. Can you tell me who it's for?'

'Yes,' he replies, still trying to restrain the Doberman, 'it's for my mother-in-law. You see, Brutus here attacked and killed her.'

'I'm very sorry to hear that,' he says. 'Um, it's probably not the time to ask, but do you think I could *borrow* your dog?'

The mourner jerks his thumb over his shoulder and says, 'Get to the back of the queue, mate.'

A duck goes into a chemist shop and waddles up to the counter. 'Hello there little fella, what can I do for you?' asks the pharmacist.

'I'd like a box of condoms,' quacks the duck.

'Not a problem,' says the pharmacist. 'Would you like me to put them on your bill?'

'What kind of a duck do you think I am?' the duck replies.

A woman wakes up one morning to find a recently escaped gorilla up her tree. Looking through the Yellow Pages, she finds Gorillas 'R' Us Removal Service: no ape too small.

Pretty soon the gorilla guy arrives armed with a stick, a pit bull terrier, a shotgun and a pair of handcuffs. His instructions to the woman are: 'I'm going to climb up the tree and poke the gorilla with this stick until he falls out of the tree. When he does, the pit bull will bite him on the testicles and the gorilla will then cross his hands in pain, allowing me to handcuff him.'

'What do I do with the shotgun?' asks the woman.

'That's to shoot the pit bull if I fall out of the tree before the bloody gorilla!' he replies.

Jesus, Moses and this really old guy are playing golf one day. The first hole is a five hundred and ten metre par five over a lake. Moses is first to tee off. He tops his tee shot, his ball racing towards a watery grave. Quickly, Moses raises his club, the water parts and his ball rolls through to the fairway safe and sound.

Jesus is next to tee off. He plays a similarly bad shot. Just as his ball is about to splash into the middle of the lake, Jesus gesticulates and the ball suddenly hovers about two centimetres above the surface of the water. Jesus walks across the lake and chips it back safely onto the fairway.

The old guy then tees off, hooking his tee shot so badly, it flies over the fence onto the road and into some oncoming traffic. It bounces off a truck and hits a tree. From there it bounces onto the roof of a house adjacent to the fairway, rolls into the gutter and then down the spouting into a drainage channel and back towards the aforementioned water hazard. As it's about to roll back into the lake, it hits a stone, bounces into the air and lands on a lily pad where it finally comes to rest. Just then a frog leaps out of the water and grabs the golf ball in its mouth and, just as he's about to leap back into the water with it, an eagle swoops down, grabs the frog with his feet and flies off. The frog drops the ball in fright, it lands on the first green and rolls gently into the hole for an 'Ace'.

Moses turns to Jesus and says, 'Geez I hate playing golf with your dad!'

Three women are sitting outside the clubhouse after a round of golf one hot day having a cool drink. Suddenly, a naked man wearing nothing but a paper bag over his head streaks past them. Upon recovering her composure, the first lady says, 'Well at least I know it wasn't my husband.'

The second woman says, 'And it definitely wasn't my boyfriend.'

'In fact, he isn't even a member of the club!' says the third.

A seven-year-old is hauled up before the headmistress to explain his absence from school the previous day. 'What have you got say young man?' she demands.

'Well Miss,' says young Johnnie, 'my grandpa got burnt.'

'Oh dear, I hope he wasn't too badly hurt,' says the headmistress.

'Too right Miss,' replies Johnnie, 'they don't stuff around at those crematoriums.'

Bloke walks into a bar with his pet monkey and orders a beer. Whilst he's drinking, the monkey slips his leash and goes berserk, running around the bar, grabbing handfuls of peanuts off the counter and eating them, and drinking all the slops out of unattended glasses. He then leaps onto the billiard table, grabs one of the balls, stuffs it into his mouth and swallows it whole. The proprietor is naturally enough furious and demands an explanation from the monkey's owner. 'Yeah, I'm sorry about that, the little bugger is a bit uncontrollable and tends to eat anything he can lay his hands on. I'll pay for the billiard ball and any damage he's caused,' says the monkey's minder.

A couple of weeks later, he returns with the monkey and orders a beer. The monkey climbs up onto the counter, grabs a maraschino cherry from an empty cocktail glass, sticks it up his bum and then eats it.

The proprietor is disgusted. 'Did you see what your monkey just did then? He stuck a cherry up his bum and then ate it. Why does he do that?'

The monkey's owner replies, 'Well, ever since he ate that billiard ball he makes sure he measures everything before he eats it now.'

For three years, a young barrister had made an annual trip to Bendigo doing 'circuit' work for his firm. On each trip he would stay at his favourite family hotel and, on his most recent trip, had finally consummated an affair with the owner's voluptuous young daughter. A year went by and it was time for his fourth trip. As he trudged up the stairs to his room, there was the hotelier's daughter at the top of the stairs nursing a beautiful little baby – the spitting image of the barrister. 'Dorothy, why didn't you write or call when you found out you were pregnant,' he cried, 'I would have rushed back here to marry you and the baby would've had my name.'

'Well,' said Dorothy, 'when I found out I was pregnant, I sat up all night with Mum and Dad and we talked and talked for hours. It was then we all decided it would be better to have a bastard in the family than a lawyer.'

Two bees meet each other on a daisy one sunny afternoon. 'So, how was your summer?' asks bee number one.

'Lousy,' says bee number two. 'Too much rain, too cold, hardly any flowers and not nearly enough pollen.'

'Gee, I'm sorry to hear that. I had a terrific summer,' says number one bee. 'I tell you what though, I've just heard that the Goldberg family bar mitzvah is this afternoon and it's just around the corner. Why don't you drop in – should be plenty of flowers and fruit there.'

'Hey great idea, thanks!' says bee number two.

An hour later, the bees bump into each other again. 'So, how was the bar mitzvah?' asks bee number one.

'Great!' says bee number two.

'But what's that on your head?' asks bee number one.

'It's a yarmulke,' says bee number two, 'I didn't want them to think I was a WASP.'

A priest and a nun are on their way back from a trip to the country when their car breaks down. It's late at night and they can't get it fixed until the morning. They walk back to the nearest town where the lone hotel has only one room available. 'Sister, I don't think the good Lord would be too worried, under the circumstances, if we spent the night together under the one roof. I tell you what, you can have the bed and I'll sleep on the couch,' says the priest.

'I can't see a problem with that,' says the nun.

Ten minutes after they've settled in their agreed sleeping locations, the nun whispers, 'Father, I'm terribly cold – you couldn't get me a blanket, could you?'

'Certainly sister, it would be my pleasure,' obliges the priest.

Twenty minutes later, just as he's nodding off, he hears the nun say, 'Father, I'm still very cold, could I have another blanket?'

'OK sister, I'll get another blanket for you,' says the priest, now becoming just a little agitated.

Ten minutes later, she's at it again. 'Father, I'm still terribly cold. I don't think the Lord would mind if just once we acted as man and wife for just one night,' she says.

'Great idea,' says the priest. 'Get your own bloody blanket then.'

Three Indian squaws were preparing for the births of their first child. The first squaw laid out a large deerhide by the river. The second squaw laid out a large bearhide under a tree by the river. The third squaw laid out a hippopotamushide by a path near the river and the tree – the three forming a triangle.

As coincidence would have it, the three women all gave birth on the same day. The squaw on the deerhide had a five kilogram son, the second squaw on the bearhide had a six kilogram son, while the third squaw on the hippopotamushide gave birth to an eleven kilogram son. In doing this, these women also gave birth to the first proof of the Pythagorean theorem, which as we all know is: 'The son of the squaw on the hippopotamus is equal to the sons of the squaws of the two adjacent hides.'

Three Frenchmen are discussing the definition of the expression *sang froid* which (as we all know) is french for 'coolness' or 'cold blood'. The first Frenchman says, 'Zat eez easy. *Sang froid* eez when a man walks into 'is bedroom and finds 'is wife in bed with 'is best friend. If he can turn around and quietly close ze door without them knowing he was there, *that* is *sang froid*.'

The second Frenchman says, '*Non, non, non*. You 'ave eet all wrong. *Sang froid* is when you walk in and say, "excuse me, please continue".'

'You are both wrong,' pipes up the third Frenchman. 'It is when you walk into ze room and say, "Excuse me, please continue," and eef they can continue − *that* is *sang froid*!'

An Aussie tourist in a Spanish restaurant asks for the house specialty. When it arrives, he asks the waiter what kind of meat it contains.

'Ah *señor*, these are the *cojones*,' the waiter declares proudly.

'And what, pray tell, are the *cojones*?' asks the tourist.

'They are the testicles of the bull killed in the ring today *señor*,' says the waiter without blinking an eyelid.

The tourist, not wanting to seem like a wimp, reluctantly eats the dish and, to his surprise, finds it quite tasty. Returning the following evening, he orders the same dish. After finishing his meal, he calls the waiter over.

'Was there a problem *señor*?' asks the waiter.

'Not really Manuel, but the *cojones* did seem a little smaller today.'

'Ah yes *señor*,' says the waiter, 'you see, sometimes the matador . . . he loses.'

America, Japan and Russia each decide to send an astronaut up to the Mir space station for a two-year mission. In a major departure from tradition, and because it's going to be such a long stretch, they agree that each astronaut can take up any sort of entertainment weighing up to eighty kilograms.

The American asks NASA if he can take his seventy-kilogram wife. They agree.

The Japanese guy has always wanted to learn to speak Greek and understand all the great Greek philosophers. He requests eighty kilograms of books on the subject. Not a problem, says NASA.

The Russian, not wanting to pass up such a golden opportunity for a little Western decadence and self-indulgence, requests eighty kilograms of the finest Cuban cigars. You got it, says NASA.

They're all finally shot into space and two years later arrive safely back on Earth. A huge crowd is gathered at Cape Canaveral to welcome the astronauts as they step off the space shuttle.

Obviously the American had a lot of fun, as he appears with his wife holding a brand-new infant.

The Japanese guy then fronts the microphone and thanks everybody in perfect Greek, quoting Socrates.

Then it's the Russian's turn. Slowly he mounts the rostrum, grabs the lectern with one hand, a half-chewed Cuban cigar in the other, and as his knuckles slowly turn white, seethes through clenched teeth, 'I don't suppose anyone's got a match?'

A fellow packing his clubs into his boot is accosted by his wife. 'Where do you think you're going?' she demands.

'I thought I'd get eighteen holes in before dinner,' he pleads in a pathetic tone.

'Haven't you forgotten we have to visit your mother in hospital this afternoon? You can play nine holes and that's all,' says the wife.

Reluctantly, the husband agrees and upon finishing his truncated round, is loading his clubs back into his boot when he spies an old girlfriend walking through the carpark. They renew acquaintances and she suggests they go back to her apartment for a session of torrid lovemaking.

Against his better judgement he agrees and subsequently arrives back home very late with his wife standing at the front door, rolling pin in hand and a little storm cloud over her head with rain, thunder and lightning coming out of it. 'And where do you think you've been? Your mother is so angry with you – not to mention what I'm going to do to you! What have you got to say for yourself?' she bellows.

Realising he's been caught out, the husband decides to confess all and tells his wife of his infidelity and every sordid detail of what he and the ex-girlfriend got up to throughout the afternoon.

She looks at him for a few moments, then, without warning, starts flailing him with the rolling pin screaming, 'You lying bastard! You played eighteen holes, didn't you!'

Murphy is staggering home from the pub late one night with a flask of Scotch in his hip pocket. He slips over on the rain-sodden footpath, falling on his backside and breaking the bottle. As he staggers to his feet and feels the Scotch trickling down his leg, he looks up to the heavens and says, 'Oh God, please tell me that's blood!'

Murphy walks into a pub. His mate Seamus O'Leary says to him, 'So how did your date with young Kathleen go last night?'

'Oh it was great,' says Murphy, 'I took her out dancin', then we had supper in the town and then we went to lover's leap for a bit of canoodling.'

'So what happened Murphy, come on details lad!' says O'Leary.

'Well I asked her for a kiss and she said first I'd have to put the top down on the car. It took me nearly two hours.'

'Two hours!' exclaimed Seamus. 'Geez Murphy, I can put my top down in three minutes.'

'Ah yes,' says Murphy, 'but you've got a convertible!'

Prince Charles arrives for an official visit to Alice Springs – the temperature fifty degrees in the shade. Charles is dressed in a light cotton safari suit and sandals. But strangely, atop his head, is a hat made from fox fur.

The mayor of Alice Springs can't help but notice the royal noggin is sweating rather profusely and, as they're sitting there reviewing a parade specially put on for the prince, he leans over and whispers, 'Er, beggin' your pardon Your Royal Highness, but why are you wearing that hat on such a hot day?'

'Oh this?' says the prince. 'Well you see, when I told the queen I was coming out to Australia, she asked me what my first port of call was. When I told her Alice Springs, I think she said, "Where the fox hat!"'

———

Two retired Jewish gentlemen bump into each other in Cavill Avenue, Surfers Paradise. 'Abe! How have you been?, asks Moe. 'It's been twenty years if it's a day. How's Rachel and the kids?'

'Fine, just fine,' says Abe, giving his friend a huge hug.

'You must come and have dinner with me and Ruthy, she'd love to see you and Rachel again,' enthuses Moe.

'We'd love to,' says Abe. 'Is this Wednesday OK? Where do you live?'

'Well, we've got a lovely apartment on the fifty-fourth floor of Seaview Towers, just down the road from Seaworld. It's number 456 Surfers Parade. To get to our floor, all you have to do is get in the lift and push the button with your nose.'

Puzzled, Abe asks, 'Push the button with my nose? Whatever for?'

'After all these years, you're arriving empty handed?' says Moe.

———

A Jewish kid asks his father for fifty dollars.
'Forty dollars! What do you need with thirty dollars?' says the father.

———

Two partners in a Melbourne business have a beautiful secretary. After some time the inevitable happens and not one, but both partners start fooling around with her and she eventually becomes pregnant. Panic-stricken, in her eighth month they bundle her off to Noosa to have the baby.

Some months go by and they don't hear a word from her so one of the partners decides to fly up and check things out. The next day he rings his partner back in Melbourne. 'Dave, there's good news and bad news up here,' he says.

'What's the good news?' Dave asks.

'She had twins!'

'What's the bad news?'

'Mine died,' he replies.

Teacher begins sex education with her class of ten-year-olds. 'Now today children, we're going to discuss *positions*. Now do any of you know about positions?'

Little Johnnie raises his hand and says in an excited voice, 'Please Miss, I know a hundred positions.'

Nervously, the teacher says, 'Er, I don't think we've got time to discuss a *hundred* positions right now so if any other children know just one or two . . .'

Looking around the room and realising she's not going to get an answer, she says, 'Well, I guess I'll start off. Let's begin with the most common position where the man's on top and the lady's on the bottom.'

Suddenly, little Johnnie starts frantically sticking up his hand.

'Yes Johnnie?' says the teacher.

'That,' says Johnnie, 'makes one hundred and one!'

Two elderly pensioners at a doctor's surgery. 'Doc, we're having a bit of trouble with our sex life. Would you mind terribly taking a look at what we're doing and maybe come up with some suggestions?' asks the old man.

The doctor replies, 'Well I'm not really a sex therapist, but if you insist, I'll give it a try.'

After watching the elderly couple making love, the doctor says, 'From what I can see, there doesn't seem to be anything wrong. In fact, I wish my sex life was as good. I really can't give you any suggestions for improvement.'

With that, the couple depart but they're back again with the same request three weeks running.

After the third week, the doctor finally says, 'Now listen you two, you aren't having any trouble with your sex life at all, are you? This is your idea of kinky sex, isn't it?'

The old guy replies, 'Well actually no, doc. You see if we have sex at my house, my wife will find out. If we have sex at her house, her husband might catch us. The motel down the road charges fifty dollars per half day and we can't afford that. You only charge thirty-five dollars and Medicare pays half of it!'

It's 1960 and a magazine journalist is sent by his editor to America to do a feature story on the life and times of the famous American general, George Armstrong Custer. On arrival, he is told that there is an ancient Indian chief still alive who actually lived through the experience with an amazing ability to remember, down to the most minute detail, everything that ever happened to him.

The journalist tracks the old Indian down to a reservation in the Midwest and starts to grill him. 'On what day of the week did Custer's last stand take place?' he asks.

'Wednesday,' replies the chief.

'What was Custer wearing when he died?'

'A black uniform, ceremonial sword, brown boots, one heel slightly worn.'

'OK,' says the journalist, becoming a little suspicious, 'what did Custer have for breakfast that morning?'

'Eggs,' answers the old chief.

By now, the journo is very sceptical and decides that anyone could make up answers like these so he leaves and the article is never published.

By coincidence, ten years later, on another assignment, the journalist finds himself passing through the same area of the reservation and decides to drop in on the old chief.

As he spies him squatting outside his tepee, he raises his hand and says, 'How!'

'Soft boiled with chips and bacon on the side,' says the chief.

Bloke rushes through the front door of his house and shouts to his wife, 'Rowena, pack your things! I've just won lotto!'

Rowena replies, 'Fantastic! Should I pack for warm weather or cold?'

He replies, 'I don't care what you do. Just so long as you're out of my life by midday!'

A bloke's marooned on a desert island that is slowly sinking into the ocean. As the water is starting to lap around his feet, suddenly a motorboat appears. 'Get into the boat, your troubles are over,' says the boatman.

'No thank you,' says the castaway, 'I have faith in the Lord. He will save me.'

The boat departs, the water continues to rise and yet another boat arrives. 'Get into the boat or you'll drown,' says the second boatman.

Again, he refuses saying, 'Go away, I have faith in the Lord. He will save me.'

The boat duly departs and by now the water is up to his chin as a third boat arrives. 'Get in man, this is your last chance!' pleads the boatman.

'No, no! God will save me.'

The boat leaves him and, of course, he drowns.

On reaching Heaven, he is greeted at the pearly gates by God. 'Hey God,' he says, 'I trusted you all my life and you let me drown . . . I don't believe it!'

'*You* don't believe it?' says God. 'What about the three bloody boats I sent?!'

A woman in her mid-fifties is undergoing hormone replacement therapy and becomes a bit concerned. So much so, she decides to visit her doctor.

'What seems to be the problem Mrs Jones?' asks the doctor.

'Well doctor,' says Mrs Jones, 'there seem to be some weird side effects – I'm starting to grow hair all over my chest.'

'Hmmm, that seems a little unusual. Why don't you take off your blouse and we'll take a little look, shall we?' says the doctor.

Upon removing her blouse, the doctor is shocked, 'Goodness me Mrs Jones, you're right. You do have hair all over your chest. How far does it go down?'

'All the way to my balls, doc. Which is another thing I need to talk to you about!'

A bloke's out duck hunting. He shoots a duck and starts wading out to claim it when he's confronted by an American also out duck shooting.

'That's my duck!' says the Yank.

'Oh no it's not,' says the Aussie, 'I shot it. It's *my* duck!'

The argument goes back and forth for a few minutes until the Aussie says, 'Now listen hear you Yankee ponce, let's settle this the Australian way.'

'How does that work?' asks the Yank.

'Well, it's traditional in cases like this that the first person to claim a disputed dead duck (you in this case) has to allow the other party to kick him in the groin as hard as he can. Then, it's the other bloke's turn. This continues until the last man standing claims the duck.'

'OK Aussie, seems fair enough,' says the American, standing with his legs apart and his arms folded in front of him. 'Give it your best shot.'

The Aussie takes a few steps backwards and then with a flying leap kicks the American in the groin so hard, he immediately doubles up in agony and falls to his knees, tears of pain streaming from his eyes.

Dragging himself to his feet, the American finally regains his composure and says to the Aussie, 'OK pal, now it's my turn.'

The Aussie gives a dismissive wave of his hand and says, 'Nahhh . . . keep the duck!'

A young bloke walks into a chic furrier in Toorak with a magnificent blonde on his arm. 'Would you kindly show this young lady the finest mink you have in the shop,' he says.

The owner of the shop goes out the back and produces an absolutely gorgeous full-length coat. The blonde is totally knocked out as she tries it on. As she's admiring herself in the mirror, the owner sidles up to the young fellow and whispers, 'I hope sir realises this particular item is worth over seventy thousand dollars.'

'Not a problem,' he whispers back, 'I'll write you a cheque.'

'That would be fine sir,' says the owner. 'But as today is Friday, you'll have to call in Monday to pick up the coat when your cheque has cleared.'

The young chap and woman leave and on Monday he returns to the store where an outraged owner says, 'That cheque you gave me on Friday is totally worthless – it bounced! Where on Earth do you get the gall to show your face in here?'

'I just had to come by and thank you for the most wonderful weekend of my life,' he grins.

Murphy walks into a bar and orders three pints of Guinness. The bartender brings him three pints and Murphy proceeds to take a sip from each one in turn until all three glasses are empty. He then orders three more.

The bartender says, 'Sir, I know you like them cold, but you don't have to order three at a time. I'll keep a bit of an eye on you and, when I see your glass getting low, I'll bring you a fresh one.'

Murphy says, 'No, you don't understand. Y'see, I have two brothers – one in Australia and the other in New Zealand. Before they left, we made a pact that every Friday night we'd still have a drink together. At this very moment, my brothers are also having three Guinnesses, so you see, we're drinking together.'

'What a wonderful tradition!' exclaims the barman.

This ritual of ordering three stouts went on for weeks and weeks until one Friday night Murphy came in and ordered only two.

As Murphy is sitting there taking a sip from each glass, the bartender, summing up the situation, says to Murphy in a sympathetic tone, 'I know your tradition and if I'm not mistaken one of your brothers has died. You have my deepest sympathy.'

Murphy answers, 'Oh me brothers are fine. It's just that I've given up drinking.'

Seamus and Murphy are walking past a pub in Northern Ireland when there's a huge explosion. A bomb has gone off and a head rolls out of the front door. 'Begorrah Seamus!' says Murphy, bending over and picking up the head, 'I'm sure that's Patrick O'Donnelly!'

'No, not possible,' says Seamus. 'Patrick was much taller than that.'

An American tourist wandering through Dublin airport comes across Murphy standing beside a long trestle table with a sign that reads: 'Famous Irish skulls'.

'Are these skulls genuine?' asks the American.

'To be sure they are sir – all skulls of the most famous Irishmen that ever lived sir,' replies Murphy.

'Fantastic!' says the American. 'Just take me through some of the names.'

'Well sir,' says Murphy, 'this one here's James Joyce the famous author, and this is Michael Collins the leader of the 1916 uprising, then we have St Brendan the navigator and my pride and joy sir, St Patrick – the patron saint of Ireland, God bless his soul.'

'Hey, I've gotta have St Patrick. How much do you want for him?' says the Yank.

'It pains me to let him go sir, but I could let you have him for a mere fifty pounds sir,' says Murphy.

The American pays up and, along with his newly acquired treasure, boards his flight back to the United States.

Five years later, the same American is wandering through the same airport and sees Murphy in the same spot with the same trestle table and an assortment of skulls. Smelling a rat, the American asks Murphy to go through his spiel again. When Murphy reaches the skull of St Patrick, the American stops him and says, 'Just a second you little swindler, I was here five years ago and you sold me a skull of St Patrick. The one you've got there is much smaller than the one I've got.'

'Ah yes,' says Murphy, 'but this is St Patrick when he was a boy.'

One sunny day a priest was taking a walk through a forest when he came across a sad-looking little frog sitting on a toadstool.

'Why are you so sad?' asked the priest.

'Well,' said the frog, 'the reason I'm so sad on this beautiful day is because I wasn't always a frog.'

'Fascinating,' said the priest. 'Please tell me more.'

'Well, you see once upon a time I was a choir boy at the local church. I too was walking through this forest when I was confronted by a wicked witch. "Get out of my way," I yelled. But, yell as I might, she wouldn't let me pass and became so angry, she cast an evil spell on me and turned me into the frog you see before you.'

'How tragic,' said the priest. 'Is there no way this spell can be reversed?'

'Yes,' replied the frog. 'It is said that if a kindly soul would take me home, provide me with food and warmth and a good night's sleep, I would wake up a boy once more.'

'Well little frog, this is your lucky day,' said the priest as he picked the little frog up and took him home.

The priest gave the frog lots of food, placed him by the fire and then, at bedtime, placed him on the pillow beside him.

When the priest awoke the next morning, lo and behold – there was a choir boy . . . And that ladies and gentlemen of the jury, is where the defence rests its case.

A married couple arrive at their golf club for a round – she with the girls, he with the boys. A young bloke walks up to the husband and asks if he needs a caddy for the day. The golfer agrees and the boy is duly hired.

As the husband is about to play his second shot on the par four sixteenth, he asks his caddy, 'What club should I use here?'

'Hmmm, about 158 metres, I'd suggest a five iron, sir,' says the caddy.

The shot veers badly towards the adjacent fairway and as fate would have it, his wife is about to play her shot and is hit in the head with the wayward ball and killed instantly.

Her funeral takes place a few days later and it's months before the husband can bring himself to walk onto a golf course. Eventually, with the help of his friends, he is convinced to take up once again the game he loved so much.

Coincidentally, on his return, he meets the same caddy. When they reach the fateful par four sixteenth on his second shot the husband once again asks his caddy what club he should use.

'Hmmm,' says the caddy, 'it's about 158 metres – I'd suggest a five iron, sir.'

'You stupid little idiot,' says the husband, 'the last time you suggested that, I didn't even make the green!'

Paddy and Sean are sitting in a hotel having a drink and watching television. On the news, there is coverage of a woman threatening to jump off a building. Paddy says, 'Tell you what, Sean, I'll make a bet with you. If she jumps, I get twenty dollars, if she doesn't, you get twenty dollars.'

'You're on,' says Sean.

The woman jumps and kills herself and Sean forks over his twenty dollars.

A few minutes later, Paddy turns to Sean and says, 'My conscience has got the better of me, I can't take this twenty from you. That was a replay – I actually saw it on the news earlier this afternoon.'

'No, no,' replies Sean. 'You keep the money, you won it fair and square. You see, I saw it on the television earlier, too.'

'You did?' asks Paddy, 'Well why did you bet the woman wouldn't jump?'

'Well,' says Sean, 'I didn't think she'd be stupid enough to do it twice!'

Blind chap walking along a city street with his guide dog. They stop at some traffic lights and the dog suddenly lifts his leg and pees on his owner's trousers. The blind chap reaches into his pocket, pulls out a dog biscuit, bends over and gives it to the dog.

A fellow pedestrian who's been observing all this, walks up to the blind man and asks him why he's rewarding his dog for such a dastardly deed.

'Oh I'm not rewarding him,' says the blind man, 'I'm just finding out where his head is so I can give him a kick up the backside.'

———

Eighty-three-year-old Maurie Goldberg. He goes into the confessional at St Patrick's Cathedral.

'Have you anything to confess?' asks the priest.

'Indeed I do Father,' says Maurie, 'Ruth, my wife of fifty years, died a couple of months ago and I have since met a beautiful twenty-six-year-old blonde girl. I have been sleeping with her every day since we met and sometimes we make love two or three times a day.'

'And how old are you?' asks the priest.

'Eighty-three,' replies Maurie.

'Tch tch,' says the priest. 'I suggest you go home and say ten Hail Marys.'

'Hail Marys?' says Maurie. 'I can't do that, I'm Jewish.'

'Then for God's sake, why are you telling me all this?' asks the priest.

'I'm telling everybody!' says Maurie.

———

'The first student,' says the teacher, 'who can tell me who the greatest man who ever lived was can have the rest of the afternoon off . . . Yes Mario?'

'Please Miss, I think it was Michelangelo.'

'Well,' says the teacher, 'he was a very great man but I don't think he was the greatest man who ever lived . . . Yes Mary?'

'Please Miss,' says Mary, 'Sir Winston Churchill?'

'He was indeed a very great man Mary but not the greatest man who ever lived,' says the teacher.

With that, from the back of the room, young Bernie Epstein raises his hand and says, 'Jesus Christ!'

'Very good Bernie, that's quite correct. You may have the rest of the afternoon off.'

As Bernie is leaving the classroom, the teacher calls him over to her desk and says quietly, 'You know Bernie, given the fact you're Jewish, I'm very surprised you said *Jesus* was the greatest man who ever lived.'

'Well Miss,' says Bernie, 'We all know it was actually Moses . . . but business is business!'

Two mates are camping in the outback. It's the middle of the night and they're both asleep in their tent when all of a sudden one of them lets out a yelp of absolute agony. As his friend awakes, he sees a snake slithering away out of their tent.

'That bloody snake just bit me on the bum!' cries the victim. 'Quick, find the nearest phone find out from a doctor what we should do!'

With that, his friend runs a couple of kilometres down the road until he finds a phone box. Gasping what happened into the phone, he asks the doctor on the other end for instructions.

'Well,' says the doc, 'you must go back to your friend as quickly as possible, cut a little "X" with a penknife where he was bitten and suck out the venom – but do it quickly or else he'll die.'

'Thanks doc,' he says and runs back to the camp site.

Relieved at seeing his friend return, the other camper says in a panic-stricken voice, 'Well, what did the doctor say?'

'Sorry mate, he says you're gunna die!'

Little Jewish kid in class at around Christmas time: The teacher announces that once again this year there will be a Christmas pageant and everyone must participate, no matter what their religion.

Young Nathan Goldstein is panic-stricken at being selected to tell the story of how Christ was born.

'It's OK Nathan dear, I'll help you,' says his mother on hearing the news. 'What I'll do is write little clues to help you remember just inside the top of your underpants – so don't worry, you won't be embarrassed.'

The night of the pageant arrives and it's Nathan's turn on stage. Nervously he begins, 'Once upon a time there was a lady called um, er . . .' Looking down furtively, he unfolds the top of his underpants on his left-hand side and says, 'Mary! And she was married to a man called um, er . . .' Again, he looks down, unfolds the top at the middle of his underduds and says, 'Joseph! And they had a little baby called . . .' Again, he folds down his underpants on the right-hand side and declares in a proud voice, 'Calvin Klein!'

Bloke walks into a bar with his German Shepherd and orders a beer and some cigarettes.

'Sorry mate, we haven't got any fags,' says the barman.

'That's OK,' he says, 'I'll get Prince here to run across the road to the milk bar. Prince, here's fifty dollars, nip across the road to that milk bar and get me a packet of Marlboro.'

The dog takes the fifty dollars in his mouth and departs.

The barman is amazed. 'Hey, that dog is really something! Is he really going to bring some cigarettes back for you?'

'Sure,' says his owner, 'he can do all sorts of stuff, he is one amazing dog.'

Half an hour goes by and his owner is now getting a little concerned. All of a sudden they hear a screech of brakes. He and the barman race outside and there's Prince making mad, passionate love to a very attractive poodle in the middle of the road.

'Prince! I'm very disappointed you. You've never done this before!' yells his owner.

'Fair go' says the dog, 'I've never had fifty bucks before!'

Young Adolf has not spoken a word for years – in fact since the day he was born. Try as they may, Mr and Mrs Hitler cannot get a word out of him no matter how hard they try. They take him to doctors, child psychologists, even speech therapists but not a word does he utter.

One day, at the breakfast table, just after young Adolf's fifteenth birthday, his mother places two slices of toast on a plate in front of him. Adolf takes a bite . . . then, to the astonishment of his mother, says, 'The toast is cold.'

'Adolf my darling, you spoke, you spoke!' cries Mrs Hitler. 'But why have you waited all this time?'

'Up until now,' says Adolf, 'everything was perfect.'

A priest in small country town takes Cardinal O'Connor on a tour of his tiny parish. Walking along the main street, they see a family of eight walking together. Turning to the priest, the cardinal says, 'Now there goes a good Catholic family.'

'Yes indeed,' says the priest proudly, 'the father is one of my ushers and the mother teaches in our Sunday school.'

Strolling a bit further on, they come across an even larger family. 'Now there's another fine Catholic family, Father,' says the Cardinal.

'My word. The twins are both altar boys and their aunt is a Benedictine sister,' says the priest.

As they turn the corner, they espy yet another large family – a mother, father and seven children. 'This is fantastic,' enthuses Cardinal O'Connor, 'another good Catholic family.'

'Well actually Your Eminence,' whispers the priest, 'that family is Presbyterian.'

'Bloody sex maniacs!' says the Cardinal.

Two elderly Catholic nuns are sitting at a football match at the S.C.G. watching the Sydney Swans play the West Coast Eagles. Two drunken yobbos sit down behind them. 'We'd better go to Melbourne next time we wanna see a game – there won't be any Catholics watchin' footy in Melbourne,' says one yobbo.

'Yeah,' says the other one in an equally loud voice, 'or maybe we could go to Adelaide, 'cos I don't reckon there'd be any of those bloody Catholics watchin' footy there.'

'Nahh! I reckon we oughta go to Tassie – there won't be any Catholics watchin' footy down there,' they persist.

Finally, losing her patience, one elderly nun turns and says with a smile, 'Why don't you both go to Hell – I'm sure there won't be any Catholics there either.'

A white kid and a black kid are in the playground debating whether God is black or white. The argument rages for an hour until the white kid finally says, 'Look Leroy, there's only one way to find out, let's ask him.' With that, young Johnnie looks towards the heavens and says, 'Oh heavenly father, pray tell us – are you black or are you white?'

Suddenly there is a clap of thunder and a voice booms from above, 'I am what I am!'

'See, that proves it!' says young Johnnie.

'How do you figure that?' asks Leroy.

'Well, if God was black, he would've said: "Ah is what ah is!" '

Three couples in their seventies, fifties and twenties, are getting ready to join the Catholic church. After spending a month completing the formalities, the instructing priest takes them aside and tells each couple that there is one remaining test of faith they must endure and that is to abstain from having sex for two weeks.

The two weeks finally elapse and each couple is called into the priest's office to receive their certificate of Catholicism. 'How did you go abstaining from sex for two weeks?' he asks the couple in their seventies.

'Not a problem – it was a breeze,' says the elderly gentleman.

'Well then, welcome to the Catholic church,' says the priest.

The couple in their fifties go through the same questioning with a similar response, 'Welcome to the Catholic church,' beams the priest.

Then it's the turn of the young couple in their twenties. 'Well then you two, how did you cope with no sex for two weeks?' asks the priest.

Shamefaced, the young man says, 'Look Father, we must be completely honest with you. The first two or three days weren't a problem but, as each day went by, we were overcome more and more with lust for each other until one day I saw Kylie bending over the freezer and, overcome with desire, I made love to her right there and then.'

'In that case,' said the priest, 'you're not welcome in the Catholic church.'

'That's OK,' replied the young man, 'we're not welcome in Safeways anymore either.'

A missionary is working with a cannibal tribe, attempting to convert them to Christianity. One day, the cannibal chief's wife gives birth to a bonny bouncing baby boy. One problem – it's white. The cannibal chief is incensed and orders the cooking pot to be made ready as he storms into the missionary's hut demanding an explanation – convinced the missionary has had something to do with it.

Trying to calm the enraged chief down, the missionary says to him, 'Look chief, the Lord works in mysterious ways. Now, see all those white sheep on the hill?'

'Yes,' says the chief.

'Now, see that one little black sheep?'

The chief suddenly looks all knowing and whispers to the missionary, 'OK, you've got a deal – I no tell if you no tell!'

Bluey, Luigi and Murphy are sitting together high atop a construction site in the city eating their lunch. 'Bloody hell! Not cheese and pickle sandwiches again!' moans Bluey.

'Mama mia, notta bloody salami sandwiches again,' complains Luigi.

'Jasus and all, not Vegemite again!' says Murphy.

'Fair dinkum, if my missus gives me cheese and pickle again tomorrow, I'm gunna kill myself,' says Bluey.

The others agree.

The next day, sure enough, they've all got the same lunch so one by one, they jump to their deaths.

Later at the wake, Bluey's wife sobs, 'If only I'd known he hated cheese and pickle, I would have made him something else – he only had to say.'

'Poor Luigi,' cries Maria, 'if only he had told me he hated salami.'

'Oh my poor dear Seamus!' sobs Mrs Murphy, 'if only I hadn't let him make his own lunch that day!'

Victor Smorgan is granted a private audience with the Pope. 'Your Holiness,' he says, 'I've heard the church has had some financial reverses of recent times and I'm willing to donate two hundred million dollars to the cause – in return for one small favour.'

'Certainly my son,' says the Pope. 'And what would that be?'

'Well,' says Victor, 'that part of the Lord's Prayer where it says, "Give us this day, our daily bread" – I would like you to change it to, "Give us this day our daily meat."'

The Pope is somewhat taken aback. 'A very unusual request Mr Smorgan, but a very generous donation. Let me put it to the college of cardinals and I'll get back to you with an answer in a few days.' As soon as Victor leaves, the Pope leans into his intercom and says, 'Monsignor Alberto, I think we might have to review the Sunicrust account.'

A man stumbles into a bar in Dublin and asks the only other patron there if he can buy him a drink.

'Why of course,' comes the reply.

The first man asks, 'Where are you from then?'

'I'm from Ireland,' says the second man.

'You don't say, I'm from Ireland too! Let's have a drink to Ireland then.'

'Of course,' replies the second man.

The first man says, 'So where in Ireland are you from?'

'Dublin,' comes the reply.

'I can't believe it – I'm from Dublin too. Let's have a drink to Dublin too.'

Curiosity overcomes the first man and he asks, 'What school did you go to?'

'St Marys,' says the second man. 'I graduated in 1964.'

'This is unbelievable!' says the first man. 'I went to St Marys and I graduated in '64! Let's drink to St Marys as well.'

By this time, the two men are rolling drunk and making a lot of noise laughing and reminiscing.

One of the regulars walks in and asks what's going on.

'Oh nothing much,' says the bartender. 'Just the O'Shaunessey twins getting drunk again.'

———

Murphy is walking along a beach and finds a lamp. He gives it a rub and a genie appears. The genie tells Murphy he can have three wishes. Murphy thinks for a moment and says, 'Firstly, give me a bottomless mug of lager.'

Poof! A mug of lager appears in his hand.

Murphy takes a sip which is magically refilled. Murphy keeps sipping and the mug keeps getting refilled until he is pissed as a parrot.

The genie, becoming a little impatient, says to Murphy, 'And what about your other two wishes, sire?'

Murphy thinks for a moment and slurs, 'OK, give me two more mugs just like this one!'

———

A young priest is sitting beside an old rabbi in a light plane travelling between some country towns. 'Rabbi,' says the priest, 'have you ever thought of changing sides?'

'What do you mean my boy?' asks the rabbi.

'You know, becoming a Roman Catholic. It really is the best religion – chosen in the eyes of God and all that,' enthuses the young priest.

'My boy, I have been Jewish all my life. Why, at eighty-three should I even think of becoming a mick? There's about as much chance of that happening as there is of this plane reaching the moon.'

The young priest persists, extolling all the virtues of his chosen religion, but still the rabbi resists.

All of a sudden there's a loud explosion and the plane starts plummeting to the Earth. The pilot deftly manages to bring it down in a paddock but, on landing, the plane flips over throwing the priest one hundred metres clear. Looking back at what's left of the plane, he sees the old rabbi stumbling out of the wreckage, dusting himself off, and then making the sign of the cross.

Elated, the priest runs up to the rabbi and says, 'Oh thank God, I finally convinced you to convert.'

'What in the hell are you talking about? asks the rabbi.

'I just saw you make the sign of the cross,' says the priest.

'Cross, schmoss!' replied the rabbi. 'I was just taking inventory – spectacles, testicles, wallet and watch!'

A young, innocent married couple on their wedding night – neither has ever seen the other naked before. She has undressed in the bathroom and is already under the covers as her new hubby begins to disrobe. As he takes off his trousers, she notices that both his knees are pockmarked and quite red. Upon her asking, he replies, 'Oh yes, you see when I was a child, I had the kneezles.'

Then he takes off his socks and she sees that his toes are horribly deformed. 'What happened to your feet?' she asks.

'When I was a boy, I suffered from tolio,' he says.

Then, he takes off his underpants. She takes one look and says, 'No, don't tell me – smallcox?'

A Catholic priest, an Anglican minister and a rabbi are discussing how much money their respective churches collect each week and how they divide it up. The priest says, 'I have a very simple method – I draw a line on the floor, throw all the money into the air and whatever lands on my side is mine and I give whatever lands on the other side to God.'

'Ah yes, I have a very similar method,' says the Anglican minister, 'except I draw a circle and whatever lands in the circle I keep and outside the circle goes to God. Now rabbi, what do you do?'

'Well,' says the rabbi, 'I throw all the money into the air – and whatever stays up, he keeps.'

St Peter questioning three men before he admits them through the pearly gates: 'Now fellas,' he says, 'welcome to Heaven. The latest innovation up here is that everyone gets a car to get around in. The quality of the car is very dependent on how faithful you were to your wives back on Earth. We'll start with you young man,' he says, addressing the first chap. 'Were you true to your wife?'

'Yes I was St Peter – I never strayed once from the day we were married,' says the young man.

'Well here are the keys to that brand new Rolls-Royce over there – congratulations,' says St Peter. 'Now how about you – were you faithful to your wife?'

The second bloke says, 'Well, I must admit, early in our marriage I did stray once or twice but I never did it again and I loved my wife very deeply.'

'A very honest reply my son,' says St Peter, handing him the keys to a brand new Ford Fairlane.

Then it's the third bloke's turn. He's a shocker. 'I'm sorry St Pete, I'm an absolute disgrace. I slept around from day one. I wasn't fussy – anything that had a pulse or walked upright. I couldn't help myself but, all through it, I made sure my wife never found out as I really did love her very much.'

St Peter frowns and then, in a forgiving tone says, 'Well, you have at least been honest and you did love her so I'll let you have this ten-speed bike to ride around on. In you all go.' He opens the gates and the three men enter.

Sometime later, the bloke on the bike is riding along and sees the fellow in the Rolls parked at the side of the road sobbing his heart out. 'Hey mate! You got the Roller – what have you got to cry about?' asks the cyclist.

'I just saw my wife go past on a skateboard,' he sobs.

A factory worker has his left ear severed in an industrial accident and is rushed to hospital.

'I'm afraid there's very little we can do for you as far as transplants go Mr Smith,' says the doctor. 'We're right out of human left ears but we do have a pig's ear just arrived yesterday.'

'Well, anything's better than nothing, doc, let's do the operation,' says Mr Smith.

The operation is performed successfully and the pig's ear takes immediately. After a couple of days in hospital, the doctor tells the worker he may go home but to come back in a couple of weeks for a check-up.

Two weeks later, he's back in the doctor's surgery. 'So, how's your hearing?' asks the doctor.

'Pretty good doc,' he says, 'I can hear perfectly out of my right ear . . . But I'm getting crackling in the other!'

Murphy is walking along the street sporting the biggest black eye you've ever seen, when he meets his good friend O'Leary.

'Moi, dat's quite a shiner you've got there, Murphy. How in God's name did you get it?' asks O'Leary.

'Well,' says Murphy, 'I was coming out of the doctor's this morning and came across Bernie O'Brien who asked me where I'd been. I told him I'd just been to the doctor to give him a specimen. O'Brien asks me, "What's a specimen?" I told him, "You go piss in a bottle" . . . And he said, "Oh yeah? And I go spit in your eye!" And that's how the fight started.'

Murphy is working in a sawmill when he accidentally saws his ear off. It falls on the ground amongst all the sawdust. His workmates frantically start looking for it so they can rush him off to hospital to have it sewn back on.

Suddenly, O'Shaunessy yells out, 'I've found it, I've found your ear Murphy!'

133

Murphy takes one look at it and says, 'No, that isn't my ear – mine had a pencil behind it.'

Jesus is out playing golf at Royal Melbourne with St Peter one sunny afternoon. Standing at the tee, Jesus says to St Peter, 'What do you think I should use here, a wood or an iron?'

'I'd use an iron for safety,' says St Peter.

'Not on your nellie. Greg Norman would use a wood,' says Jesus.

'I'd think again if I were you, Jesus,' says St Peter. 'If you use a wood, you'll finish up in that trap on the left.'

'I still think Greg Norman would go with the wood,' says Jesus and proceeds to tee off. Of course, his ball finishes up in the bunker.

Upon reaching the trap, St Peter says to Jesus, 'I think the safe play here is to lay up with an eight iron – if you try and make the green from here, you'll probably finish up through and into that lake behind it.'

'I reckon Greg Norman would probably use a five iron and go for the green,' says Jesus.

'Suit yourself J.C.,' says St Peter, 'but I still think the best bet is the eight iron.'

With that, Jesus smites the ball a beauty, it bounces onto the green and into the lake behind. On reaching the green, Jesus walks across the lake to retrieve his ball.

As he's doing so, a member comes up to St Peter and says, 'Who does that bloke reckon he is – Jesus Christ?'

'Naah,' says St Peter, 'he thinks he's Greg Norman!'

An Aussie digger is captured in the desert by Rommel's troops during World War II. He is brought before the German commandant who says, 'We decided that you will be executed as a spy, but you can walk free if you can complete three tests we will give you. If you don't complete them successfully, you will die anyway. What is it to be?'

The Aussie, figuring he's got nothing to lose says, 'OK, I'll do the three tests. What are they?'

'See those three tents?' says the commandant. 'For test number one, you will go into the first tent where you find five bottles of schnapps. You must drink each bottle until it's empty. For test number two, you must go into the second tent where you will find a ferocious lion with an impacted wisdom tooth. You will remove the tooth with your bare hands.'

'Crikey!' says the digger. 'What's the third test then?'

'In tent number three, you will find a beautiful woman who has not been made love to for over ten years. You will stay in her tent until her cravings are completely satisfied. If you complete all three tests, you are a free man,' says the commandant.

With that, the Aussie goes into the first tent and about an hour later comes staggering out and zig zags his way into the second tent. All of a sudden, there is a gigantic roar from the lion, the walls of the tent begin to flap furiously as it rocks from side to side. After about five minutes of roaring and crashing, the digger comes staggering out. He weaves his way up to the commandant and slurs, 'OK Fritz, now where's that sheila with the impacted wisdom tooth?'

A bloke goes to his doctor who tells him he's only got twelve hours to live. On arriving home, he tells his wife who, naturally enough, bursts into tears.

'Darling,' she sobs, 'I'm going to make this a night you'll never forget. We'll go out to the best restaurant in town and, when we get home, you can make love to me as often as you like.'

After a wonderful, expensive meal at an exclusive restaurant, they crawl into bed and have a mad, passionate lovemaking session. Just as she's about to fall asleep, he taps her on the shoulder and says, 'Darling, that was fantastic, can we go again?'

They get stuck into it again and, just as she's falling asleep again, she feels the tap on the shoulder. 'One more time honey?' he asks.

'Hey! Give me a break!' she says, '. . . *you* don't have to get up in the morning.'

The prime minister of Israel, visiting the president of the United States, is invited into the Oval Office. On the president's desk he sees a red phone and a white phone. 'What's the red phone for?' he asks.

'Well sir,' says the president, 'that's my direct line to the Russian president in Moscow and this white one is my direct line to God.'

'Wow!' says the Israeli prime minister, 'a direct line to God – how much does a phone call to God cost?'

'Oh,' says the president, 'about five thousand dollars a minute.'

The Israeli leaves, very impressed.

A couple of months later, the US president is visiting the Israeli prime minister and notices three phones on his desk.

'The blue phone is my direct line to you, Mr President,' says the PM. 'This red phone is my direct line to the Kremlin, and this white phone is my direct line to God.'

'Hmmm,' says the president. 'Out of curiosity, how much do you pay for a call to God?'

'Twenty-five cents a call – no time limit,' says the Israeli PM.

'Twenty-five cents!' exclaims the president. 'How come it costs me five thousand dollars a minute to talk to God and you only twenty-five cents?'

'Well you see,' explains the PM, 'from here, it's only a local call.'

A Frenchman, a German and a chap named Murphy have all been found guilty of murder in fifteenth-century France and are sentenced to death by guillotine.

As they place the Frenchman face down in the device, he closes his eyes and says a prayer as the executioner pulls the lever. Just as the lethal blade is about to behead him, it suddenly stops about ten centimetres from his neck.

The crowd start cheering, 'Spare him! Spare him! It's God's will!' With that, the Frenchman is set free.

Then it's the German's turn. Exactly the same thing happens and he is set free.

Now it's Murphy's turn. As he's led up the stairs, he says to the executioner, 'Hang on a minute, do think I'm crazy? I'm not getting into that thing until they fix it!'

───────

Two Hollywood producers speak on the phone: 'Saul, it's Jerome, what's happening?'

'Everything Jerome, everything. I just sold a screenplay to Warner for half a million, I just got a hundred thousand dollar advance from my publishers for my next novel and NBC have said yes to my latest sitcom series.'

'OK,' says Jerome, 'I'll call back when you're alone.'

───────

A cat and a mouse walk into a café and sit down in a booth near the window. When the waitress arrives, the mouse says, 'I'll have a plate of cheese and a couple of bread rolls please.'

'And what will your friend have?' asks the waitress.

'He won't have anything,' says the mouse.

'But isn't he hungry?' persists the waitress.

'Look lady, if he was hungry,' says the mouse, 'do you think I'd be still sitting here?'

───────

Bloke sticks his head over his neighbour's fence and sees him digging a hole. 'What are you doing, Blue?' he asks.

'I'm burying my budgerigar, Dave,' says Bluey.

'Bloody big hole for a budgerigar, Bluey,' says Dave.

'Not really,' says Bluey, 'it's inside your cat!'

───────

A bloke's setting up a sundial in his front garden when his neighbour calls in. 'What's that, Harry?' asks his neighbour.

'Well, Frank,' says Harry, 'when the sun hits this small triangular spike, it casts a shadow on the face of this flat piece of stone. Then, as the sun moves across the sky, the shadow also moves across the calibrated dial, enabling me to tell what time it is.'

'Jeez, what'll they think of next,' says Frank shaking his head.

Two young boys are playing in a school yard when one asks the other if he knows what a penis is. The kid says he doesn't know but he'll ask his dad that night.

After dinner that night, the young lad gets his father aside and says, 'Dad, what's a penis?'

'Son, not only will I tell you what a penis is,' says Dad, 'but if you come into the bathroom, I'll *show* you what a penis is.'

They go into the bathroom and dad drops his dacks, proudly declaring, 'Son, that's a penis! In fact, not only is that a penis – it's a perfect penis!'

Next day at school, the lad finds his friend and they go into the boys' toilets together. He lowers his shorts and says to his mate, 'See this? This is a penis. Not only is it a penis, if it was two inches shorter, it would be a perfect penis.'

Two women are playing golf. One tees off and to her horror, she hooks her ball so badly, it strikes a man on the next green. He immediately clasps his hands together over his crotch, doubles over and then proceeds to roll around on the ground in agony.

The woman rushes up to him to apologise and says, 'It's OK, I'm a physiotherapist and I can relieve the pain if you'll let me.'

'Owwww!' cries the victim as he remains in the foetal position. With that, she begins to gently massage his groin.

After a few moments, she asks, 'Does that feel better?'

The bloke looks up and says, 'Yes, that does feel pretty good . . . But my thumb still hurts like billyo!'

Roland and Sam are playing golf. After twelve holes it becomes quite obvious that Roland isn't having a very good day.

'Hey Roland, you don't seem to be your old self today. Is anything wrong?' asks Sam.

Glumly, Roland replies, 'I think Martha's dead.'

'That's terrible,' says Sam. 'You think your wife is dead – aren't you sure?'

'Well,' responds Roland, 'the sex is the same, but the dishes are piling up.'

A barrister arrives in Heaven and knocks on the pearly gates.

'Ah,' says St Peter, 'Mr Donoghue, we've been expecting you – welcome to Heaven.'

'But this isn't fair,' says the barrister. 'I'm only forty-five and far too young to die.'

'Hmmm, that's odd,' says St Peter rubbing his chin. 'According to the hours you've billed, we've got you at one hundred and twenty years old.'

A lawyer drives through a red light and prangs into a doctor going through on the green. Shaken, the doctor staggers from his car. The lawyer pulls a flask from his pocket and offers the doctor a drink, which he gratefully accepts.

'Aren't you going to have one?' asks the doctor as the lawyer recaps the flask and puts it back in his hip pocket.

'Sure,' says the lawyer. 'Just as soon as the police have finished breath testing us both.'

After a very hard year, Denis decides to take a long break on Hamilton Island. Relaxing on a sun lounge beside the pool, he spies an old university chum doing the same. 'Ross me old mate! I haven't seen you in yonks. What are you doing with yourself these days?' he beams.

'Well actually, I'm practising law,' whispers Ross. 'But don't tell mother – she still thinks I'm a pimp.'

A struggling young lawyer is sitting in his threadbare office waiting for the phone to ring when suddenly there's a knock at the door. On opening it, he is confronted by the devil, who says in an evil voice, 'I have an offer to make.'

Somewhat shaken, the lawyer says, 'OK, anything would be better than this – go ahead.'

'I will increase your income five-fold, your partners will love and trust you, your clients will respect you, you will have five months holiday every year, always drive the latest Mercedes and you'll live to be one hundred and five. All I require in return is your wife's soul, your children's souls and their children's souls. They must all then rot in Hell for eternity.'

'Hang on, hang on,' says the lawyer, 'what's the catch?'

Four eminent surgeons are discussing their work over lunch. First surgeon: 'I like operating on accountants. You open them up and everything inside is numbered.'

Second surgeon: 'I much prefer operating on librarians. When you open them up, everything is in alphabetical order.'

Third surgeon: 'Well, electricians are the easiest to operate on. When you open them up, everything inside is colour coded.'

Fourth surgeon: 'Personally, I like operating on lawyers. They are heartless, spineless, gutless . . . And their heads are interchangeable with their dicks!'

A Hindu, a rabbi and a lawyer are driving through the country late one night when their car breaks down. They walk a few kilometres until they come across a friendly looking farmhouse. When they knock on the door, the farmer explains that he only has two beds so one of the three will have to sleep in the barn with the animals.

The rabbi offers to sleep in the barn and let the other two have the beds. Ten minutes later, there's a knock on the bedroom door. They find the rabbi standing there exclaiming, 'I can't sleep in that barn; there's a pig in there! It's against my religion to sleep in the same room as a pig.'

So the Hindu offers to sleep in the barn. Ten minutes later, there's another knock on the bedroom door. It's the Hindu standing there this time saying, 'I can't sleep in the barn either, there's a cow in there and it's against my religion to share the same room as a cow.'

The lawyer, anxious to get a little shuteye, pipes up and says he doesn't have a problem sleeping with animals and departs for the barn.

Two minutes later there's a knock at the bedroom door, the rabbi opens it to find the pig and the cow standing there.

A young lady is sitting in a lawyer's office. 'I'm very worried about the cost of consulting you. How much would you charge if I asked three questions?' she says.

'Two hundred dollars,' says the lawyer.

'Two hundred dollars!' exclaims the young lady. 'Is that ethical?'

'It certainly is,' says the lawyer. 'Now, what was your third question?'

Murphy and O'Leary arrive at the football ground to see their favourite team play. Just as they're walking away from their car, O'Leary says, 'Damn it Murphy! I've locked my keys in the car.'

'What are we going to do?' asks Murphy.

'I don't know. Perhaps if we break the windshield we'll get them out.'

'No, that's a bit drastic,' says Murphy. 'Maybe we could find a coathanger and open the door that way.'

'Well,' says O'Leary, 'We'd better think of something fast because it's starting to rain and the top's down.'

Murphy gets a job with the C.S.I.R.O. experimenting on animals. His first job involves a frog. Placing it on the table, he says in a very loud voice, 'Jump frog, jump!' He records the distance, cuts off one of its legs, then yells again, 'Jump frog, jump!' He records the distance, cuts off a second leg, shouts the same instructions and once more records the distance. The experiment continues in the same way until the frog is lying on the table with no legs at all – just the torso. Murphy shouts, 'Jump frog, jump.' Nothing. He yells even louder, 'Jump frog, jump.' Still nothing. Murphy then writes out his summary of the experiment:

'With four legs, frog jumps one metre. With three legs, frog jumps seventy centimetres. With two legs, frog jumps thirty centimetres. With one leg, frog jumps seven centimetres. With no legs, frog goes completely deaf!'

A gorilla walks into a pub, sits on a stool, whacks ten dollars on the bar and orders a Bundy and Coke.

The barman is flabbergasted and, in shock, gets the gorilla's order, takes his ten dollars and gives him one dollar change.

After a few minutes, when he's recovered his composure, the barman works up enough courage to make some small talk with the gorilla. 'Um . . . er,' he stumbles, 'we don't get many *gorillas* in here these days.'

'At nine bucks for a Bundy and Coke, I'm not surprised,' says the gorilla.

A drunk's sitting at a bar in a restaurant at the top of a fifty-storey city building. He leans over to the bloke sitting beside him and slurs, 'I'll betcha a hundred dollars I can jump out that window there and then jump back in again.'

His drinking companion accepts the bet and they ask the bartender to hold the wager. The drunk lurches through the window, disappears for a few moments then, with a sudden whoosh, he comes back through the window.

The other bloke is really amazed and angry at losing his hundred dollars and says to the drunk, 'OK mate, double or nothing says you can't do it again!'

'You're on,' says the drunk and once again he throws himself out the window only to whoosh back again a few moments later.

The bloke at the bar thinks, 'He must have got lucky. I'll bet a freak gust of wind blew him back in the window – I've gotta get my money back.'

'All right mate,' he says to the drunk, 'if *you* can do it, I can do it. I'll bet you *four* hundred that I can jump out the window and come right back in.'

'OK,' slurs the drunk. 'You're on.'

Once more, the bartender holds the bet. The other drinker takes a running jump out the window, plummets fifty storeys down to the street below landing with a loud splat. Dead!

The barman leans over to the drunk and says, 'You know, you can be a real bastard when you're pissed, Superman.'

Paddy and Sean are digging a ditch which just so happens to be opposite a brothel. As they're digging, they notice a Protestant minister walk up to the front door, look furtively around and then enter the house of ill repute. 'Would you look at that Sean?' says Paddy. 'A shameful sight that is, a man of the cloth visiting such a godforsaken, unholy place. It's bloody shameful it is.'

All of a sudden, a rabbi fronts up, takes a look around and he enters the bordello.

'I don't believe my eyes!' exclaims Sean. 'No wonder the youth of today are so confused when these men of God are setting such a bad example, it's a damn disgrace it is.'

Next to enter the whorehouse is a Catholic priest.

'Ah, the pity of it all,' says Paddy to Sean, 'one of the poor girls must be dyin'.'

The most famous espionage agent in history is Murphy the spy. So famous, the CIA call on him only when there's a dangerous and important job that the president can trust to nobody else. Not only is Murphy the spy famous, but he is also the most difficult intelligence agent to locate. When he's not involved in espionage, he disappears amongst the folk of a village on the coast of Ireland.

One day, a special mission arises that only Murphy can handle. The president sends his most trusted agent from Washington to find him, armed only with Murphy's secret password, 'The weather looks fine now, but it might rain later.'

When he arrives in the village, the CIA man figures the most logical place to start his search for Murphy would be in the local pub. After a couple of beers, the agent asks the bartender, 'Do you have anyone in this town by the name of . . . Murphy?'

'To be sure we do sir,' says the bartender. 'Right next door there's Murphy the baker. He's there every day and he'd be happy to help.'

'I don't know whether Murphy the baker is the man I'm looking for. Is there anyone else called Murphy in this town,' asks the agent.

'Ah yes, there certainly is sir,' answers the barman, 'at the church at the top of the high street we have Father Murphy, a kindly old soul who'd be more than happy to –'

'I don't think he's the one either,' interrupts the agent. Looking around furtively, he asks, 'Do you by chance have another Murphy nearby?'

'Well of course,' says the bartender, 'just up the road, we have Murphy the solicitor – a very helpful chap and he's probably there right now.'

'No, no,' says the agent, 'I don't think that's him. Aren't there any *other* Murphys in this godforsaken town?'

'Actually, there are quite a few sir,' says the bartender. 'In fact my name happens to be Murphy.'

'It is?' says the agent. He moves closer to the bartender and says, 'The weather looks fine now, but it might rain later.'

'Oh,' says the bartender slapping the bar with his hand, 'you'd be looking for Murphy the spy then!'

A father and his son are walking through a park one afternoon and come across two dogs mating. 'Hey Dad, what are those dogs doing?' asks the boy.

'Well son,' replies the father, 'they're making puppies.'

That night, the young lad is feeling a little thirsty. He goes to his parents' room, opens the door and discovers them in the middle of making love. 'What are you doing?' he asks.

'Well son, we're making babies,' replies the father.

'In that case,' says the boy, 'could you turn Mummy over? I think I'd much rather have a puppy.'

A stagecoach is rumbling along a bush track when all of a sudden from behind a tree steps bushranger Ned Kelly. Waving his gun in the air, Ned says to the stagecoach driver, 'Right, you bucket of scum, I'm going to rape all the men and rob all the women.'

'Excuse me Ned,' says the driver, 'I don't mean to tell you how to do your job, but don't you mean you're going to rob all the *men* and rape all the *women*?'

Just then, an effeminate little male voice lisps from within the coach, 'Who's robbing this coach, you or Mr Kelly?'

Two musicians who have hung out together for years are involved in a car accident and one of them is killed. About a month later, the surviving muso is awakened in the middle of the night by a ghostly presence in his room. 'Who's that? Who's there?' he cries out.

'It's me, Wilbur,' says this faraway voice.

Full of excitement, he sits bolt upright in bed. 'Wilbur, Willie, is that really you? Where are you?'

'Well Daryl,' says the faraway voice, 'I live in Heaven now.'

'Wow man, Heaven!' says his friend. 'What's it like up there, dude?'

'It's really cool daz,' says Wilbur, 'I'm jammin' with the best up here every day. I'm playing with the 'Trane and the Bird and Count Basie's here – boy is he smokin'.'

'Sounds great,' says Daryl, 'tell me more!'

'What can I say?' says Willie. 'But there's some good news and some bad news up here.'

'What's the good news?'

'Well the good news is that the guys are in top form – I have never heard them sounding so tight. Man they are wailin' up here.'

'So, what's the bad news then?'

'The bad news,' says Willie, 'is that God has got this girlfriend who he says can sing a bit . . .'

———

The commander of an elite commando force is informed the president of the United States is coming to his barracks to inspect his men and to find out how tough they are. In order to impress the president, the commander invites him to visit at five o'clock in the morning in the dead of winter. Come the day, and the entire SAS company is lined up in two rows on the parade ground – totally naked.

The president is curious and asks the commander why he's putting his men through such an ordeal.

'Well sir,' replies the commander, 'I just want you to see just how much pain these men can withstand and to give you peace of mind knowing that they are battle-ready in all kinds of weather, sir.'

So the inspection begins. As they walk along the line, the commander pulls out his parade stick and gives the first soldier's penis a hefty whack. 'Did that hurt soldier?' he barks.

'No sir!' replies the soldier, wincing just a little.

'And why not soldier?' asks the commander.

'Because I'm a proud member of the SAS and we're as tough as nails, sir!' shouts the soldier.

They move on to the next soldier whose penis also cops a whack. 'Did that hurt soldier?' yells the commander.

'No sir!' bellows the soldier.

'Why not?'

'Because I'm a proud member of the SAS and we're as tough as nails, sir!'

The president is very impressed and follows this painful ritual all the way down the line until they come to the last soldier in the front row. Again, the commander gives the soldier's penis an almighty whack. The soldier doesn't even wince. 'Now come on soldier – that *must* have hurt!'

'No sir!' shouts the soldier.

'And why not soldier?'

'It belongs to the man behind me, sir!'

Private Johnson's mother dies suddenly. At the morning muster, the sergeant major has all his charges assembled in preparation for the day's activities. 'Today,' he says, 'we'll be conducting tank exercises in the abandoned quarry down the road, some of you will be doing bayonet practice and the rest will have shooting practice. And Johnson, your mother's dead. Dismiss!'

On hearing the news, Johnson bursts into tears and collapses on the floor. His mates gather around him and escort him from the drill hall.

The colonel of the regiment has been observing all of this and takes the sergeant major aside. 'I really think you could use a little more tact next time something like this happens SM Smythe. Don't you think you could break tragic news like that a little more tactfully next time? I mean Private Johnson will be mentally scarred for life.'

'Very well sir,' says the sergeant major. 'Message received and understood, sir!'

As coincidence would have it, the very next day, Private Symons's mother dies and, with the colonel's advice ringing in his ears, the sergeant major decides on a new tack the following morning. 'Now listen up you scungy lot. Today, you'll all do ten laps of the parade ground and then you'll go on a ten-kilometre forced march with full backpacks. Now, one more thing, I want all of you with mothers to take one step forward. Where do you think you're goin' Symons?!'

Two young blokes are discussing how hard it is to find the right girl to marry. 'Yeah, it's not easy,' says one. 'Every sheila I bring home to meet my parents, Mum doesn't like.'

'That's easily fixed,' says the other. 'All you have to do is bring home a girl who's just like your mum.'

'I've already done that,' he says, 'and that's the one the old man didn't like.'

An elderly man in a nursing home celebrates his ninetieth birthday. After all the relatives depart, there's a knock on his bedroom door. Upon opening it, he sees a beautiful young woman with a fabulous figure in a short skirt and stiletto heels standing there. She's a surprise gift from some of the old codger's army mates.

'What can I do for you young lady?' he asks.

'I'm here to give you some super sex,' she replies.

'Actually, I'm a bit tired after the party,' the old man says, 'I'll just have the soup thanks.'

'And another thing,' shouts the doctor to his wife as they argue over breakfast, 'you're not even good in bed.'

After storming out of the house to go to work, by midmorning he's feeling very guilty and phones his wife to make amends. After ringing for quite some, she finally answers. 'What took you so long to answer?' he asks.

'I was in bed,' she says.

'What were you doing in bed at this time of the day?'

'Getting a second opinion!'

Bloke arrives home from the pub and says to his wife, 'Harry Johnson the milkman reckons he's seduced every woman in our street, except one.'

She thinks for a couple of seconds then says, 'Yeah, probably that stuck up bitch at number forty-nine.'

Bloke wandering through a cemetery comes across a grave. The headstone reads: 'Here lies John Williams, a lawyer and an honest man.'

'How about that,' he thinks, 'three men buried in the one grave!'

A policeman pulls a couple over for speeding. 'Could I please see your driver's licence sir?' he says to the husband.

'But constable, I wasn't speeding. I was only doing fifty-eight kilometres an hour!' protests the husband.

'Well sir,' says the cop, 'I've got you clocked on my radar at seventy-five kilometres an hour in a built up zone.'

'I don't believe you,' the husband says, 'I'd like to take a look at your reading.'

'Believe me sir, you were exceeding the speed limit, now please show me your licence.'

'How do I know you're a real policeman?' asks the husband.

At this point, his wife leans across the seat and says to the cop, 'Don't worry about my husband constable, he always gets this argumentative when he's drunk.'

A drunk driving home late one night after a binge at his local hotel passes an unmarked police car. The cop decides to follow him at close range and nab him when he pulls into his drive. On arriving home, the drunk staggers from his car and attempts to put his key in the lock. The cop grabs his shoulder and says, 'Excuse me, sir, but I have reason to believe you have been driving whilst under the influence.'

'No I haven't,' slurs the drunk.

'Well sir, can you prove to me this is your house?' asks the cop.

'Sure I can, I'll take you inside and prove it,' he says.

They enter the house.

'You see constable, this is my bedroom . . . and this is my wife,' he explains.

'And who is the bloke next to her?' the policeman demands.
'Why, that's me of course!'

My psychiatrist has gone high-tech with his switchboard. These days when I ring him, I get the following messages on hold:

If you are ringing about a codependency, please get someone to press one for you.

If you are a compulsive-obsessive, please press two over and over again.

If you suffer from a multiple personality disorder, press numbers three, four, five and six.

If you are a paranoid-delusional, we know who you are and why you've phoned. Just stay on the line until we can get this call traced.

If you are a manic-depressive, well it doesn't really matter which button you press – probably no-one's going to answer anyway.

'I've got a real problem doc,' says Murphy to his psychiatrist. 'Every night I can't sleep because I keep thinking there's somebody under the bed. I get up every hour and check, sleep for a few minutes and then wake up and have to check again – it's driving me crazy, you've gotta help me!'

'Hmmm,' says his shrink, 'that really is a problem and I can't fix it in a hurry. I shall need to see you twice a week for the next year.'

'How much do you charge?' asks Murphy.

'Two hundred dollars a visit.'

'Two hundred a visit! Let me think it over,' says Murphy.

Murphy never goes back. Six months go past and he meets the doctor in the street.

'Why didn't you ever come back?' asks the shrink.

'For two hundred bucks a visit? You'd have to be jokin' doc,' says Murphy. 'My local barman cured me for just ten dollars.'

'Oh really! How?'

'He told me to cut the legs off the bed.'

It's a pitch-black night and a ship's captain suddenly sees a light dead ahead on a collision course with his vessel. He sends a signal: 'Change your course immediately ten degrees east.'

The light signals back: 'Change *yours* ten degrees west.'

The indignant captain then signals: 'I am an admiral of Her Majesty's Navy. Change *your* course sir!'

'I'm a seaman, second class,' comes the reply. 'Change your course, sir.'

By now the captain is furious. 'I'm a forty-thousand tonne battleship! I'm not changing course.'

There's one last reply: 'I'm a lighthouse – your call, dickhead!'

Rabbi Cohen has always strictly observed Jewish dietary laws. But one day, whilst sitting alone in a restaurant, he notices roast pig on the menu. 'Just once,' he thinks, 'I'd like to try it.' He calls the waiter over and places his order. The pig is brought to his table with an apple stuck in its mouth. Just as he's about to tuck in, a member of his synagogue walks in, stops in his tracks and stares at him and his meal in disbelief. 'So I ordered a baked apple,' says the rabbi, 'who knew how they'd serve it?'

A newly arrived priest is being briefed by his housekeeper on repairs that need doing at the rectory. 'Well Father,' says the housekeeper, 'your roof is in bad need of reshingling, your hot water service needs replacing and your office has rising damp.'

'Now, now Mrs O'Brien,' allows the priest, 'you've been the housekeeper here for many, many years and I've only been here for a few days. Why not say *our* roof and *our* hot water service – after all, we are a team.'

Several days later, the priest is having a meeting with the archbishop and several other high-ranking church officials. Suddenly, a terribly upset Mrs O'Brien bursts into the office. 'Father, father! You must come quickly,' she says, 'there's a mouse in our room and it's under our bed!'

A drunk staggers up to the hostess of a cocktail party and slurs, 'S'cuse me lady, but do lemons have legs?'

'Of course they don't you stupid man,' she retorts.

'Well in that case, I think I just squeezed your canary into my drink!'

An avid Collingwood fan brings his dog into a pub to watch the 'woods play the West Coast Eagles on television from Perth.

Reluctantly, the bartender lets them both settle into a quiet corner to watch the big game. Every time Collingwood kicks a behind, the dog goes crazy – barking, running and doing backflips.

'That's remarkable,' says the bartender, 'what does he do when they kick a goal?'

'Dunno mate,' says the owner, 'I've only had him for two years.'

Father O'Flaherty is playing golf with Liam Murphy, one of his parishioners.

Murphy's one-metre putt lips out and he mutters, 'Shit! I missed the bastard.'

The priest chastises him saying, 'If God hears you using that sort of language Murphy, he's going to strike you dead me boy. I suggest you try and control your emotions a little better.'

'I'm sorry Father, I'll try to watch my language in future,' says Murphy.

Eventually, they find themselves on the eighteenth green. Murphy has to hole yet another one-metre putt, he misses and grumbles, 'Shit! I missed the bastard.'

At that very moment, the sky darkens, there's a clap of thunder and a bolt of lightning strikes the priest. As Murphy stares dumbfounded at the pile of ashes that used to be Father O'Flaherty, a voice from the heavens booms, 'Shit! I missed the bastard!'

A skydiver is going for his first jump. Understandably he's very nervous.

At two thousand metres, his instructor says, 'Look, there's absolutely nothing to worry about young Roger. All you do is jump out of the plane, count to three and pull the ripcord. If that doesn't work, simply pull the reserve cord. There'll be a truck down there to pick you up. Now, off you go.'

So Roger jumps. He counts to three and pulls the ripcord . . . nothing. He pulls his reserve cord . . . nothing again! 'Bugger it!' he says, 'I'll bet that bloody truck's not down there either.'

A travelling salesman calls into a farmhouse late one night after his car has broken down and asks the farmer if he can stay for the night.

'It'd be a pleasure, mate,' says the farmer. 'But you'll have to share a room with my beautiful, voluptuous young daughter Doreen. Now, if there's any hanky-panky, you'll be in big trouble – is that clear?'

'Not a problem,' assures the salesman, 'I'm not that sort of bloke.'

Of course, as fate would have it, the salesman cannot control himself and finishes up in bed with the daughter and they begin to make mad, passionate love. The farmer hears the moaning and groaning and bursts into the bedroom, knocking the sales rep out cold.

On regaining consciousness, the rep finds himself in the barn still totally naked with his penis tightly wedged in a vice with the handle nowhere to be seen and the farmer standing there calmly sharpening the biggest carving knife you've ever seen.

Panic-stricken, the salesman says, 'Crikey! You're not going to cut my dick off are you?'

The farmer hands him the knife. 'No son, you can do that – just as soon as I set fire to the barn.'

John Blackman
Aussie Slang

If you don't buy this book you're one chop short of a barbecue!

Is your knowledge of Aussie slang sadly lacking? Are you feeling like a bandicoot on a burnt ridge, and running around like a blue-arsed fly? If so, don't chuck a wobbly, simply take a squiz at *Aussie Slang* and she'll be apples!

This literary triumph from John Blackman (previously published under the title *Best of Aussie Slang*) is the ultimate guide to the lingo of Down Under. Known to millions of Australians as 'the voice' of 'Hey Hey It's Saturday' and the alter ego of Dickie Knee, Blackman defines all the great slang and phrases that confront everyone, every day, all around Australia. Where words are inadequate, talented cartoonist Andrew Fyfe has let his dark, fertile mind run rife with illustrations.

So take a Captain Cook at this little bottler, impress the world with your grasp of the Aussie vernacular and find a special place (preferably one that doesn't flush) for this masterpiece in your house.

Pat Sheil
Olympic Babylon

SEX, SCANDAL AND SPORTSMANSHIP … THE TRUE STORY OF
THE OLYMPIC GAMES

Olympic Babylon is a wildly funny, unashamedly vitriolic and utterly
engrossing celebration of the darker side of the Olympic Games –
the quadrennial orgy of sports, nationalism and marketing that has
become the greatest show on earth.

Tracing the bizarre history of the Games from Ancient Greece to
Atlanta, *Olympic Babylon* focuses less on Olympic heroes than
Olympic weirdoes – the men who raced as women in the 1930s, the
marathon victors who gargled strychnine and brandy before the First
World War, the wrestling champion who was murdered by America's
richest fruitcake, the rower who stopped mid-race to let a brood of
ducklings cross the course in front of his boat before going on to win
gold.

Olympic Babylon gleefully records the obscene bidding process that
cities go through in order to win the Games, tells of the outrageous
marketing and sponsorship deals which make the modern Games
tick, and revels in the ever-more preposterous mascots, opening
and closing ceremonies and twisted rituals associated with the
world's biggest circus.

Above all else, *Olympic Babylon* looks affectionately at the athletes
themselves – from acts of selfless sportsmanship to outright fraud,
cheating, criminality and malice.

Olympic Babylon is the untold story of the Olympic Games –
sometimes heroic, sometimes tragic and frequently comic. For if
there is one theme throughout this book it is this – it is possible, just
possible, that love 'em or hate 'em, we have all been taking the
Olympic Games a little too seriously.

Adèle Lang and Susi Rajah
Horrorscopes
How To Spot a Bastard by His Star Sign

THE ASTROLOGY GUIDE WITH BALLS

■ Why do Aries men make funny little oinking noises?
■ When will the Capricorn guy get a life? (or at least a joke?)
■ How can a Gemini live with himself?
■ What possesses mothers to have Cancer?
■ And who the hell would want to date a Pisces?

All is revealed in this, the definitive guide to every bastard under the sun – according to his star sign. It's everything you needed to know but real astrologers were too polite to tell you.

Adèle Lang and Andrew Masterson
Bosstrology
A Guide to the Twelve Bastard Bosses of the Zodiac

WHY ARE ALL BOSSES SUCH BASTARDS?

- Whose bright idea was it to make Libra a CEO?
- When will your Scorpio supervisor let bygones be bygones and give you a good reference?
- Why does the Leo supremo keep stealing your glory?
- How come working for a Sagittarius requires so much medical cover?
- And where on earth has your Gemini manager disappeared to this time?

Essential reading for disgruntled employees everywhere, *Bosstrology* is an intimate, unbiased Guide to the Twelve Bastard Bosses of the Zodiac. It's also a handy-sized, tax-deductible reference tool that no office, shop, factory, farm or construction site should be without.

Bosstrology: A Guide to the Twelve Bastard Bosses of the Zodiac is the work-orientated follow-up to the love-obsessed *Horrorscopes: How to Spot a Bastard by his Star Sign.*